T0284140

# Hold
## on to
# Hope

DEVOTIONS FOR WHEN
LIFE DOESN'T MAKE SENSE

# Hold
## on to
# Hope

Sheila Thomas

BARBOUR
PUBLISHING

# Introduction

Who doesn't need hope these days? Sometimes life just doesn't make sense. Things can spiral down, and it may seem like the world is off its axis. But God offers hope throughout His Word. No matter what is happening, He assures us that He will be with us and help us through every situation.

When we read His Word, our minds can be set at ease, and we can sense His peace. God knew we would need a Savior from sin and death in this world, so He took care of it by the death, burial, and resurrection of His Son, Jesus. Then He sent us His Holy Spirit.

Now He wants us to avail ourselves of His provision by going to His Word daily, meditating on it, and getting it ingrained in our hearts and minds. Then when hard times come, we will be prepared. The more we convince our minds and hearts that He is a good Father, the easier it will be to remain hopeful and at peace, knowing He is working on our behalf to bring all things together for our good (Romans 8:28).

# Choose to Hope

*Why am I discouraged? Why is my heart so
sad? I will put my hope in God! I will praise
him again—my Savior and my God!*

PSALM 42:11 NLT

---

The psalmist David certainly had his moments of discouragement. When he had those feelings, he acknowledged them, but then he went to the Lord and chose to put his hope in Him. David loved to praise the Lord, and that praise lifted him out of the doldrums.

We all need to follow David's example at times. When our minds start to spiral down, our spirits get discouraged. But David found that the answer was in putting his hope in God and making a decision to lift his voice in praise to God his Savior.

If you find yourself down in the doldrums today, lift your voice in praise to God. Hope in Him because He never fails.

Thank You, Father, for always providing what
I need and keeping me focused on You and Your
promises. I will choose to praise You. Amen.

# *We Abide in Him*

*By this we know that we abide in him and he
in us, because he has given us of his Spirit.*

1 JOHN 4:13 ESV

---

We are never alone. We abide in God, and He abides in us. This is because He has given us His Holy Spirit. The Holy Spirit is our comforter. He is in us to give us all we need to get through every situation that arises in our life.

Remind yourself today that where He abides there is no fear, no worry, no reason for concern. Meditate on the fact that the God of the universe, who created the whole world and everything in it, lives in you. His Holy Spirit will give you guidance for everything you need.

Father, I thank You that I have the Holy Spirit because You abide in me and I abide in You. Thank You for giving me all the help that I need. I depend on You today. And I trust You fully. In Jesus' name, amen.

# Forget the Past

*No, dear brothers and sisters, I have not achieved it,
but I focus on this one thing: Forgetting the past and
looking forward to what lies ahead, I press on to reach
the end of the race and receive the heavenly prize for
which God, through Christ Jesus, is calling us.*

PHILIPPIANS 3:13–14 NLT

---

Sometimes we feel disheartened and discouraged. But take heart! Have hope! Forget the past and whatever worries or troubles are making you feel down. Instead, look forward to what is ahead.

Paul had to do that. He knew he had many failures in his past. He had actually even killed Christians. But he decided to forget his past and look forward to his future. He wanted to press on and get his heavenly prize. He knew it would be best to move on and look forward, not backward, and do his best with God's help. We can and should do the same.

Lord, today I choose to stop looking back at my failures.
I choose to stop thinking thoughts of negativity.
I choose to look at Your promises. I trust You. Amen.

# Hope Is Never Lost

*For we are saved by hope: but hope that is seen is not hope: for what a man seeth, why doth he yet hope for?*

ROMANS 8:24 KJV

---

It's obvious that we don't hope for something we already have. That wouldn't make any sense. So we hope for something we do not yet have. All real hope is in something that is not yet seen.

What are you hoping for today? Does it feel like you've been waiting for a very long time? Hang in there, because hope is never lost. Put your hope and trust in Jesus, the one who promised to always be faithful. If you find yourself telling God how you need Him to answer that prayer, stop. Rest in the fact that He knows what is best. He has your best interest at heart. Put your hope and trust in His perfect plan for your life. He is God, and He is always good.

**Help me, Lord, to stop telling You how to answer my prayers. Help me to rest in Your perfect plan. I will stay hopeful and at peace.**

# We Can Hope in Confidence

*Faith shows the reality of what we hope for;*
*it is the evidence of things we cannot see.*
HEBREWS 11:1 NLT

---

If you're longing for something, praying and believing God for answers to your prayers, you can stand strong in confident faith knowing that He will provide. The Word promises this—that God will give you everything you need.

Hoping isn't just kind of wishing for something. Using your faith brings your hopes into reality. Stand firm in God's Word. Build your faith. Thank God ahead of time for answered prayer. He will reward your faith. In His time, He will come through—we can stand on that. He always keeps His promises, and He cannot fail. He is GOD!

**Thank You, Lord, for always keeping Your promises. I stand in faith believing You will provide everything I need for my life.**

# True Hope from the Lord

*May the God of hope fill you with all joy and peace and believing, so that by the power of the Holy Spirit you may abound in hope.*

ROMANS 15:13 ESV

You may say, "I have lost all hope. You don't know what I've been through." But God is the giver of all hope. And He will fill you with all joy and peace. He will help you "abound in hope." What a beautiful thought! Through the power of the Holy Spirit, we can have great hope.

Fill your mind and thoughts with His great power. His great love. His purpose for you. What are your talents and abilities? Put your focus on how He has equipped you and what He can do through you. Do something for someone else. Be a blessing to someone who has it worse than you. You'll be amazed at how your day and your whole mindset will change for the better.

Thank You, Father, for empowering me with true hope in You. You are the giver of real hope and peace through the Holy Spirit. I choose to put my thoughts on You today.

# Hope Will Not Disappoint

*And this hope will not lead to disappointment. For we know how dearly God loves us, because he has given us the Holy Spirit to fill our hearts with his love.*

ROMANS 5:5 NLT

---

The world's hope is not founded on the real truth. That's why people are often let down and disappointed. But real, true hope that comes from God will never disappoint.

God loved us so much that He sent His Holy Spirit to fill us with love. He is the one who enables us to remain hopeful, never losing heart. We can have an expectant heart while we wait on answers from the Lord.

Put your hope and trust in Him. Realize how much He loves you. He knows you better than anyone else on this earth does. He alone knows what you truly need and what will truly satisfy you.

Thank You, dear Lord Jesus, for loving me so much. I choose to trust in Your goodness today. I will wait patiently for Your will to be accomplished in my life.

# Hope Will
# Last Forever

*You will be rewarded for this;*
*your hope will not be disappointed.*

PROVERBS 23:18 NLT

---

Meditate on this verse from God's Word today. It's beautiful. Your future is bright. No matter what negative thoughts you may be thinking, there is purpose for you because you're still alive. And the Holy Spirit is living inside you to give you a living hope that will never fade away. Stir up those good thoughts today.

Ask the Lord to reveal His plan and purpose for your life to you. Then take the first step to fulfill that plan. Make that phone call. Send that email. Reach out. You'll feel better and be glad you did. Wallowing in self-doubt and condemnation will get you nowhere. Stop the stinking thinking and move toward the Lord. He is always there to help you. He will go with you. He will lead you. He's a good, good Father.

**Lord, I choose to move toward You today.**
**I choose to believe in Your good plan for my life.**

# God Is Working in You

*For God is working in you, giving you the desire
and the power to do what pleases him.*

PHILIPPIANS 2:13 NLT

---

We have His power in us. This is good news for today and every day. God is working in you. And He will give you the desire to do what pleases Him. But He doesn't leave you with just the desire. He gives you the power to do it too.

What a wonderful heavenly Father. He makes sure we are equipped with everything we need to succeed in life. And if we walk closely to Him, He will give us the right desires. You will find yourself desiring to do things that will please God. You won't even desire to do anything that would displease Him. You will want to honor your Father by doing His plan and purpose for your life.

**Father, thank You that You are working in me and
giving me the right desires as well as the power
to do these things. I love You, Lord. Amen.**

# God Always Hears You

*"I will answer them before they even call to me.*
*While they are still talking about their needs,*
*I will go ahead and answer their prayers!"*

ISAIAH 65:24 NLT

---

We can have great hope in the fact that God hears and answers our prayers. He answers before we even call on Him. Even while we're still running our mouths about our problems, He hears us and goes ahead and answers our prayers.

Good human parents have that heart for their children. So how much more is that the heart of our loving heavenly Father? And what's even better is that He knows everything. He knows what is good for us and what is not good for us. So we can literally rest in Him, knowing He will provide what is best for us too. It may not always be what we thought we wanted, but eventually we will see that He knew best.

Dear heavenly Father, thank You for hearing
and answering my prayers according to Your
perfect plan and purpose in my life. Amen.

# God Shows Mercy

*Yet the LORD longs to be gracious to you; therefore he will rise up to show you compassion. For the LORD is a God of justice. Blessed are all who wait for him!*

ISAIAH 30:18 NIV

---

We as human beings make mistakes and mess up in life at times. It is easy to then go into self-condemnation and start beating ourselves up. But this is when we should go to God. We don't always do that, though. We often run away from Him, thinking He's eager to punish and reject us.

However, He longs to show us grace, compassion, and forgiveness. He is there waiting for us to turn back to Him, run into His loving arms, and accept His forgiveness. And oh, what peace we have when we do this. What hope we have in Him!

> Father, thank You for showing grace, mercy, and compassion to me when I mess up. You're such a good Father. Forgive me when I mess up. I long to walk in Your path and do Your will. Amen.

# God Speaks to Us

*"Call to me and I will answer you and tell you great
and unsearchable things you do not know."*

JEREMIAH 33:3 NIV

---

When we're having a down day and feel discouraged, lonely, or depressed, God said in His Word to call on Him and He will tell us great things. Things we don't even know. He will give us comfort. What a blessing!

Or maybe it's one of those days when we're just confused about something. We can't decide what to do. We can go to our heavenly Father, and He not only hears us, but He will speak to us. He will show us wisdom. He is the great counselor. How could we ever feel hopeless when we have the Holy Spirit to comfort us? Call on Him. Pour your heart out to Him. He not only hears, but He also answers.

Father God, I praise You for being the God of
comfort and wisdom. You alone can give us exactly
what we need when we need it. You are the perfect
heavenly Father. I love You, Lord. Amen.

# Hope in Troubled Times

*"When everything is ready, I will come and get you,
so that you will always be with me where I am."*

JOHN 14:3 NLT

---

We live in a world filled with trouble. It's easy to feel afraid and wonder what our future will be like. We can easily grow concerned about our family and loved ones. What will happen to them in the future? But take heart, my friend. We have great hope for our future, because if we are believers in Jesus Christ, our future is bright. One day He will return to get us and take us to heaven. And His Word says that no mind can comprehend the glory and greatness of heaven. It's going to be beyond our imagination.

If you think heaven sounds boring, think again. God, who created you with a desire to have fun, knows exactly what will bring you happiness and joy. Never fear!

Father, I'm so grateful that I don't have to worry about my future. You are preparing something better than I can even imagine for me and all who love you. What glorious hope! What great love You have for Your children! Amen.

# God Will Complete His Work in You

*Being confident of this, that he who began a good work in you will carry it on to completion until the day of Christ Jesus.*

PHILIPPIANS 1:6 NIV

---

Maybe you feel like God called you to something. You started it, but it failed. Now you're stagnant and getting nowhere. It can be very discouraging. When this happens to any of us, we begin to doubt we really did hear God's call. Maybe we were wrong. But we were so certain back then. . .

Take heart, my friend. If God called you to it, if He began the work in you to get you ready for the calling He put in you, then He certainly will complete it. He promised. Give it to God, and trust Him. Do the next right thing. Move forward. He will meet you there and give you wisdom and strength to accomplish what you were born to do.

Father, I will take the next step toward the calling You gave me. Thank You for giving me ideas and wisdom to fulfill Your plan for my life. In Jesus' name, amen.

# God Is My Source of Hope

*May the God of hope fill you with all joy and peace
as you trust in him, so that you may overflow
with hope by the power of the Holy Spirit.*

ROMANS 15:13 NIV

---

Have you ever lost your confidence in your ability to do something? Maybe you had a dream of something you wanted to accomplish. You started toward your goal but lost your confidence when you messed up or made a mistake while trying.

It's times like these when what we do can either make or break us.

But God's Word says He is the source of hope, and He will give us joy and peace when we trust Him. Then He will fill us with confident hope through the Holy Spirit. So call on Him. Let Him give you peace, joy, and confidence to try again. You can do it!

Father, I thank You that we can turn to You for help when we have lost our confidence. And You promised to give us strong confidence. Amen.

# God Will Be with Us in Trouble

*The warden had no more worries, because Joseph*
*took care of everything. The LORD was with him*
*and caused everything he did to succeed.*

GENESIS 39:23 NLT

---

How do you think Joseph felt? Talk about life going bad—he really had a rotten turn of events! His brothers initially wanted to kill him but ended up selling him into slavery. Then he was lied about and thrown into prison and basically forgotten. How would you feel? Most of us would be in the pits of despair.

But the Lord was with Joseph and caused everything he did to succeed. Somebody finally remembered him. He impressed the ruler and was set free and made ruler! Talk about a turnaround.

Joseph's story gives us great hope. No matter your circumstances right now, God can turn everything around for your good. Keep believing. Praise Him daily. Trust Him. And just you wait and see!

> Lord, thank You for putting the story of Joseph
> in the Bible to encourage us when we are in dire
> situations. What hope his story gives us! Amen.

# Hope for Healing

*For she thought to herself, "If I can just touch his robe, I will be healed." Immediately the bleeding stopped, and she could feel in her body that she had been healed of her terrible condition.*

MARK 5:28–29 NLT

---

There was a woman in the Bible who had suffered with a bleeding issue for twelve years. Can you even imagine? Back in those days she was considered unclean and had to stay away from people. When she heard about Jesus and His healing powers, she began to be hopeful that perhaps, just maybe, if she could get close enough to at least touch His garment, she would be healed. So that's exactly what she did.

Jesus immediately asked who had touched Him because He felt the power flow from Him. The woman was perhaps afraid that she would be in trouble for being so close, let alone touching His clothes.

But of course, she was immediately healed. After twelve years! Her hope turned into faith. And her faith in Jesus made her whole.

**Jesus, I am in awe of Your healing power. You are such a loving heavenly Father.**

# Hope for Impossible Things

*But when Jesus heard what had happened, he said to Jairus, "Don't be afraid. Just have faith, and she will be healed."*

LUKE 8:50 NLT

Jairus' daughter was very ill. He went to see if Jesus would come pray for her. While he was still waiting to speak to Jesus, a messenger from home came to him and said his daughter was already dead. Most people would lose hope at that point. And maybe Jairus did momentarily. But Jesus spoke a powerful truth to him. He told him to not be afraid but to just have faith, and she would be healed.

Then Jesus went to Jairus' house and told the girl to get up. And she did. Amazing!

We can definitely put our hope in Jesus, who has all the power to do everything we need in life. Put your hope and faith in Him and trust His ways. He knows best.

Thank You, Father, that we can definitely put our hope and trust in You! You care for us and want us to come to You with our fears and worries. So help me to do that. Amen.

# God Has Not Forgotten You

*For God is working in you, giving you the desire*
*and the power to do what pleases him.*

PHILIPPIANS 2:13 NLT

---

At times we can get discouraged with our situation and
feel like God has forgotten us. It may seem as if things
are not changing at all. But this is when we should look
to Philippians 2 and take heart. We can encourage ourselves in the Lord knowing that God is working in us. He
has promised to give us the desire of our hearts and the
power to do what pleases Him.

In the meantime, while we're waiting, we may need
to spend some time seeking His will to be sure that what
we are desiring, or what we think we need, is in line with
what He wants for us. Surrender to Him, and let Him
know that you are wanting only His will.

Lord Jesus, I surrender to Your will. And I wait in hope
and faith, knowing You are at work. Thank You, Father.

# *Lazarus' Sisters*

*Jesus told her, "Your brother will rise again." "Yes," Martha said, "he will rise when everyone else rises, at the last day."*

JOHN 11:23–24 NLT

---

When Lazarus was sick, his sisters sent for Jesus and hoped He would get there in time. Unfortunately He did not. Lazarus died. So Mary and Martha went ahead and buried their brother.

Death seems so final. In this case, it was not. When Jesus told Martha that Lazarus would rise again, Martha thought He meant at the resurrection. But Jesus had a different plan. He went to Lazarus' grave and called the man to come forth. And Lazarus walked out of the tomb!

We don't always know or understand God's plans. So it pays to remain hopeful and trust Him. In this case, God's plan was better than just making Lazarus well. Jesus wanted to show God's great power by raising him from the dead.

Always remain hopeful. Stay in faith. Believe God. His plans are perfect.

**Father, You are good—always good. Amen.**

# He Cares about You

*Give all your worries and cares to
God, for he cares about you.*
1 PETER 5:7 NLT

In times of fear and despair and even hopelessness, there is still hope. There is an answer for us. The Lord says to give all your worries to Him because He cares about you. And our brothers and sisters in Christ are going through some of the same things we are. We are not alone.

Jesus Christ conquered sin, hell, and the grave, so He is our victorious Savior. He will take care of us now and every time we call on Him. He promised, and He never fails.

Heavenly Father, help me to remember that I am not alone and that others are going through the same thing. You have promised to take care of me in every situation. I put my faith, hope, and trust in You today. I lean hard upon You, Father. I trust in Your Word and Your love for me. I love You, heavenly Father. Amen.

# Stand Strong
## in the Fire

*"The God whom we serve is able to save us.*
*He will rescue us from your power, Your Majesty."*
DANIEL 3:17 NLT

---

Even though Shadrach, Meshach, and Abednego were being forced to serve the pagan gods and worship the gold statue that Nebuchadnezzar had set up, they were determined to not bow. They had hope that their God, the one true God, would deliver them. But even if He didn't, they made it clear to Nebuchadnezzar that they would never give in.

These three brave men had a very earnest expectation that their God would deliver them.

It seemed as though God was not going to deliver them. They were thrown into the blazing hot furnace, which Nebuchadnezzar had made seven times hotter than usual. But a fourth man showed up!

When the king saw this, he ordered them to be brought out. They didn't get burned and did not even smell like smoke. God delivered them.

**Lord, help me stand strong in hope and faith in**
**You during the difficult times in my life. Amen.**

# What Was She Thinking?

*But when she could no longer hide him, she got a basket made of papyrus reeds and waterproofed it with tar and pitch. She put the baby in the basket and laid it among the reeds along the bank of the Nile River. The baby's sister then stood at a distance, watching to see what would happen to him.*

EXODUS 2:3–4 NLT

---

When Pharaoh ordered every newborn Hebrew baby to be thrown into the Nile River, Moses' mother hid him for three months. But when he could no longer be hidden, she put him in a basket and dropped him into the Nile River hoping he would be all right. Miriam, his sister, stayed close by and watched.

Sometimes we have to just do the hard thing and trust God. What hard thing are you going through right now? Just do the next right thing and put your hope and trust in God. He took care of Moses, and He will take care of you.

**Heavenly Father, thank You that I can put my complete hope and faith in You to take care of me in my difficult situations. Amen.**

# Even in the Belly of the Whale

*"But I will offer sacrifices to you with songs of praise, and I will fulfill all my vows. For my salvation comes from the LORD alone."*

JONAH 2:9 NLT

---

Sometimes we get ourselves into a whale of a lot of trouble (pun intended). Jonah did. He was running from God. But he found out that it was better to do God's will.

Have you ever been like Jonah and found yourself in a lot of trouble? Maybe you knew what God was asking of you, but you were unwilling to do it. So you chose another way, not God's way.

Jonah cried out to the Lord in hopes that He would deliver him. And the Lord did. He will deliver you too. All you need to do is call on Him. Ask His forgiveness. He will make everything right. He is a forgiving Father.

**Thank You, Lord, for Your forgiveness and guidance. I choose to do Your will, Lord Jesus. Amen.**

# God Will Deliver

*And the LORD was pleased with the aroma of the sacrifice and said to himself, "I will never again curse the ground because of the human race, even though everything they think or imagine is bent toward evil from childhood. I will never again destroy all living things."*

GENESIS 8:21 NLT

---

Noah had great faith in the voice of the Lord. He heard God's instructions and followed them completely. He built the ark exactly as God instructed. The people were making fun of him, so Noah was probably hoping he wasn't going to look like a fool.

But after Noah's complete obedience, God sent the rain. Forty days of it. By then, Noah was surely hoping all that rain would stop! Can you even imagine being in a boat for forty days and nights with all those animals?

Again God kept His word and delivered Noah and his family. He will deliver you too.

**Father God, thank You for being my deliverer.
I put my complete hope and faith in You. Amen.**

# What Den Are You In?

*Daniel answered, "Long live the king! My God sent his angel to shut the lions' mouths so that they would not hurt me, for I have been found innocent in his sight. And I have not wronged you, Your Majesty."*
DANIEL 6:21–22 NLT

---

There may be times in this fallen world when we will have to take a stand for what is right. Daniel had to do that. He made the decision to continue worshipping the one true God, even though the king had forbidden it. As a result, he was thrown into a den of lions.

We have to be strong in our faith at times like this. We must have an earnest expectation that God will deliver us. He promised to never leave us. He will accompany us through the trials of life. Even if the whole world turns against us, He will be with us until the very end.

Daniel knew God would deliver somehow. He didn't know the details, but he trusted God.

Father, help me completely trust You in all
my trials and hardships. Keep me strong in
my resolve to follow You always. Amen.

# Nothing Can Separate You from His Love

*And I am convinced that nothing can ever separate us from God's love. Neither death nor life, neither angels nor demons, neither our fears for today nor our worries about tomorrow—not even the powers of hell can separate us from God's love.*

ROMANS 8:38 NLT

---

Absolutely nothing can separate you from God's love. His love is perfect, continuous, and unfailing. It never runs out. And no matter what you've done, He still loves you. You can't make Him stop loving you. People may stop loving you, but He never will.

Go to Him with all your heartaches. Tell Him all your troubles. He listens, and He still loves you. He will comfort you and give you hope and peace.

Thank You, Father, that I can come to You no matter what I have done, and You love me. I'm so grateful that You never give up on me. I'm sorry for my failures. Thank You for Your forgiveness. I love You!

# Hope Through Trials

*And at midnight Paul and Silas prayed, and sang*
*praises unto God: and the prisoners heard them.*

ACTS 16:25 KJV

---

Life sometimes brings trials and situations that are
miserable—surely being in prison was for Paul and Silas.
They were human just like we are. Yet, in the midst of
imprisonment, they chose to pray and sing praises to
God. And if you read the rest of this chapter, you'll find
out that God took care of them.

When we go through those hard times, the best thing to
do is pray and trust God. Sing His praises. Read the Word.
Put our focus on Him, not the situation. He has promised
to take care of us no matter what the situation may be.
God is bigger than anything we may have to endure.

Let Paul and Silas be your examples. Keep your hope
and trust in our wonderful heavenly Father.

**Father, thank You that I can always trust You to take care**
**of me, no matter what the situation may be. Amen.**

# Waiting on Your Answer

*When hope is crushed, the heart is crushed,*
*but a wish come true fills you with joy.*
PROVERBS 13:12 GNT

---

Do you feel like you've been waiting forever for your situation to change? For things to get better? It's easy for any of us to fall into a negative mindset and get really depressed. That's when it's so important to change our focus and, no matter how long it seems, keep our hope and faith in Jesus. If we don't, the Word says our hearts get crushed.

So let's put our thoughts on the goodness of God. Stay strong in our faith. Keep believing. The answers will come. It may not be what we thought it would be, but God knows us better than we know ourselves. He knows what will make us happy and fulfilled. We can trust Him.

Father, thank You that You know what I
need. I will trust You to fulfill in my life
what Your purpose is for me. Amen.

# Look for the Good

*As they go through the Valley of Baca they make it a place of springs; the early rain also covers it with pools. They go from strength to strength; each one appears before God in Zion.*

PSALM 84:6–7 ESV

No matter what we are going through, we should dig deep to look for the good. The idea here is for us to find the blessings even in the worst situations. It's so important to keep our thoughts on His promises and look for the good in everything.

No one likes to be around someone who always has the mulligrubs. So speak positive things, expect positive things, and in time, you'll see things turn around. This is not just positive thinking. It's God's Word.

Lord, help me to stay focused on You and Your promises.
Thank You for always working in my life to bring
about what's good for me. I trust You, Jesus. Amen.

# Rest While You Wait

*Unless the LORD builds a house, the work of the builders is wasted. Unless the LORD protects a city, guarding it with sentries will do no good. It is useless for you to work so hard from early morning until late at night, anxiously working for food to eat; for God gives rest to his loved ones.*

PSALM 127:1–2 NLT

---

Are you weary from striving so hard to make things happen? Of course, we have to do our part. But let's learn to balance our part with some rest and total trust in God doing His part. He doesn't want us to be anxious and working ourselves to death, trusting only in our own efforts. He wants to give us peace and let Him take care of us.

The Bible talks about laboring into rest (Hebrews 4:9–11 KJV). That sounds like it might take some effort on our part to learn to rest. So make that decision to learn how to rest in Him. Let Him work. Trust that He is doing His part, even when we don't see it.

**Father, I choose to rest in Your promises and trust in You. Amen.**

# Nothing Is Too Hard for God

*"O Sovereign LORD! You made the heavens and earth by your strong hand and powerful arm. Nothing is too hard for you!"*

JEREMIAH 32:17 NLT

---

If God really did make the heavens and earth by His strong hand and powerful arm (and He did!), then why do we think He might not come through for us? Nothing is too hard for Him.

If you're struggling right now with a difficult situation and wondering how you're going to get through it, make a list of all the times God provided in the past. That will encourage you and build your faith for your situation right now. He never fails. He'll provide this time too.

He loves you and has already provided a way for you. Thank Him right now for the answers that are coming. That's living by faith. Put your complete hope and trust in Him, because He cares for you.

Thank You, Lord Jesus, for always taking care
of me. You always provide what I need. I put
my hope and faith in You now. Amen.

# Consider It an Opportunity to Be Joyful

*Dear brothers and sisters, when troubles of any kind come your way, consider it an opportunity for great joy.*

JAMES 1:2 NLT

---

If it weren't a good thing to remain joyful and hopeful, the Lord would not have so strongly told us to do it. He said to consider it an opportunity for great joy when we go through trials. This is when it's especially important to know that we have a good heavenly Father. We need to be in His Word regularly and understand that He has good plans for us. Otherwise it will be even harder to stay joyful in the midst of trials.

So in the midst of your trials today, stay joyful. Stay hopeful. Remember that God is at work. And He has good things in store for you. And when life brings those trials, which it will, remember that His plans are perfect. And He is always good.

**Father, thank You that I can trust Your plan
and trust You to do what's good for me.
Help me to remain joyful. Amen.**

# All Things Work Together for Good

*And we know that God causes everything to work together for the good of those who love God and are called according to his purpose for them.*

ROMANS 8:28 NLT

---

If you are a believer, then you are probably familiar with Romans 8:28. It doesn't say that everything's going to happen perfectly in life. But it does mean that God will work all things together for our good. He can rearrange any situation. And He can give us peace while we wait.

Memorize this verse and get it firmly grounded in your heart and mind. Meditate on it. Keep a mindset of expectancy. Have confidence that God is at work. His ways are higher than our ways—in other words, His ways are better.

If a good earthly father would not bring evil to us, how much more will our heavenly Father take care of us? Trust Him.

Heavenly Father, thank You for being a good and loving Father. Help me to trust You completely and know that You are working everything together for my good. Amen.

# His Plans Are Good

*"For I know the plans I have for you," says the*
LORD. *"They are plans for good and not for*
*disaster, to give you a future and a hope."*
JEREMIAH 29:11 NLT

---

So many people think that God sends disaster to our lives. But His Word plainly says that His plans are not for disaster but for good. His plans are to give us a future and hope.

So, regardless of what situation you're going through, remember that God did not bring it to you. But He will help you through it. And He will work in that situation to bring good from it. Aren't you glad that we have such a loving heavenly Father? We must be firmly grounded in this truth.

Father, I trust You to bring good into my life in the midst of my trials in life's hard situations. I trust that You have good plans for me. And I stand against the evil one, who will try to bring disaster to my life. I worship You. Amen.

# God Knows
# Your Concerns

*The LORD will accomplish that which concerns me:*
*your unwavering lovingkindness, O LORD, endures forever.*

PSALM 138:8 AMP

---

God knows everything you are concerned about today. He will accomplish what you need. He has unwavering lovingkindness for you. His love lasts forever.

If we focus on these truths, our spirits will be lifted with encouragement and hope. Give your concerns to God today. He wants you to be at peace. Whatever your situation is, remember that nothing is too hard for God.

Aren't you glad you can trust Him every moment? Put your worries and concerns in His hands. And leave them there. You don't need to carry them with you today. . .or ever! Let God set you free from your worries and concerns.

Father God, I choose to put my concerns and worries
into Your hands right now. And I will leave them
there. I know that You are at work and will accomplish
everything according to Your plan and purpose. You're a
good heavenly Father, and I praise You for that! Amen.

# The Cure for Fear Is Faith

*Now faith is confidence in what we hope for
and assurance about what we do not see.*

HEBREWS 11:1 NIV

---

Faith is the cure for all our fears today. Having faith in God gives us confidence that what we hope for and what we don't yet see in our lives *will* come to pass according to His plan.

If you are fearful today, or if you're going through something hard, keep faith in God. Focus on His goodness. Read all of Hebrews 11. See what having faith did for all the people listed there. It will build and strengthen your faith. The Lord made sure that this chapter was in the Bible for a reason. He knew we would need it for encouragement.

Lord Jesus, I choose to build my faith today and stay hopeful until I see the answers. I will focus on You and Your goodness and Your plans for my life. And until I see these answers, I will believe You are working on my behalf. Thank You, Lord. Amen.

# Live in His Power

*For God gave us a spirit not of fear but of*
*power and love and self-control.*
2 TIMOTHY 1:7 ESV

---

The spirit of fear is never from God. Anxiety and worry never are either. Anytime we are fearful, anxious, or worried, we should not entertain those thoughts, because they come from our own insecurities.

God gives us a spirit of power, love, and self-discipline. He gives us the power to overcome those thoughts. So let's not give in to the thoughts of anxiety and fear; rather, let's give place to thoughts of overcoming our situations through the power of Jesus Christ. The same power that raised Jesus from the dead lives in us. We can overcome. God has given us power to overcome. Let's do it!

**Father, You have given me the power to overcome all spirits of fear, anxiety, and worry. Help me choose to walk in that power today and every day. In Jesus' name, amen.**

# *His Power Is All You Need*

*I also pray that you will understand the incredible
greatness of God's power for us who believe him.
This is the same mighty power that raised Christ
from the dead and seated him in the place of honor
at God's right hand in the heavenly realms.*

Did you know that the same power that raised Jesus Christ from the dead lives in you as a believer? Yes, we have that same power in us. If we truly believe that, we can overcome anything that comes our way.

God didn't put us here on this earth and then leave us to figure it out on our own. He gave us His Spirit and His Word and His power! That is incredible news! We are overcomers. Let's be examples to the world of Jesus' love and power at work in us. The world needs to see something different in us.

Father, help me to be an example to the
world. I want to live above my circumstances,
giving You praise and living in the power You
have provided for me as a believer. Amen.

# He Will Protect You

*He will cover you with his wings; you will be safe in his care; his faithfulness will protect and defend you.*

PSALM 91:4 GNT

---

No matter what may come, God promises to protect and defend us.

Picture a mother hen and her babies. She covers them with her feathers and keeps them safe. God says in His Word that He will cover us with protection too. He will defend us and keep us safe.

Think about this: the God of the universe has promised to cover you with His protection. There is no safety better than that. You can stay hopeful, trusting God in every situation of your life. God has you. He loves you. He's here with you. Always. What a beautiful thought.

Jesus, I love You and praise You for always being with me. Always protecting me. Always defending me. You're all I need. I surrender my fears to You today and trust You completely. Amen.

# The Lord Delights in You

*"For the LORD your God is living among you.*
*He is a mighty savior. He will take delight in you*
*with gladness. With his love, he will calm all your*
*fears. He will rejoice over you with joyful songs."*
ZEPHANIAH 3:17 NLT

---

When a child is afraid at night, a loving mother or father will go to their bedside and do everything possible to calm the child's fears. They might speak softly to the child and tell them how much they love them. They may also sing songs for the little one.

The above verse is beautiful because it says that our heavenly Father does the same for us. He takes delight in us with gladness. He lovingly calms all our fears. And He actually sings songs over us.

Pause and think about this. It will bring you great comfort and hope. He loves you so much.

Father God, thank You for loving me so much that
You actually delight in me, calm my fears, and
sing songs over me. You are a loving Father.

# Joy Comes in the Morning

*For his anger is but for a moment, and his favor*
*is for a lifetime. Weeping may tarry for the*
*night, but joy comes with the morning.*

PSALM 30:5 ESV

Perhaps you're going through something really hard right now. Your heart is grieving. You feel like life will never be the same again. But GOD! Take heart!

God has promised us that joy will come again. He is the God of comfort. He understands your sorrow. Lean on Him. Trust Him. Put your hope and faith in Him. He will lovingly get you through. The sun will shine again. Joy comes in the morning. Thank Him in advance. Pour your heart out to Him. He hears you. He cares.

Father God, I choose to pour my heart out to
You, and I give You all my sorrows and sadness.
I choose to believe You will give me joy again.
The sun will shine again. You are faithful. I love You.

# It's Going to Get Better

*God blesses those who patiently endure testing and*
*temptation. Afterward they will receive the crown of*
*life that God has promised to those who love him.*

JAMES 1:12 NLT

---

We can have hope in the promise of God that we will receive the crown of life. Better days are ahead. And as believers, we know where we are going. Heaven is better than we can even imagine. If we think life is good here, we have no idea what heaven will be like. We cannot even grasp it.

So if you are surrounded by life's difficulties now, remember the blessings God has promised. Stand strong in your hope and faith, and in the end, you will receive that crown of life!

Not only has He promised to get us through our situations here on earth, but He has promised great rewards for us in heaven. He is preparing that place for us now.

Father, thank You for promising to get me
through all my situations here on earth as well as
preparing a wonderful place for me in heaven.

# You Have a Savior

*I will sing to you, O LORD, because you have been good to me.*
PSALM 13:6 GNT

---

At the beginning of this psalm, David was really down. He told God he was hurting. He asked God how much longer he would have to endure. How much longer would God look the other way when he needed Him? David was really depressed.

But before the chapter ends, David had changed his thinking. He chose to sing a song of joy to the Lord. He praised God for strengthening his soul. He convinced himself that he knew he had a Savior in God his Father.

Sometimes we have to do this too. We have to choose to not listen to our stinking thinking and instead focus on God and His love for us. That's how we overcome. Nobody said it was easy, but it works. It's God plan.

> I worship You, Father! You are my Savior
> and will always pick me up when I lift my
> hands to You in surrender. Thank You!

# Trusting God Is Worth It

*Trust in the LORD with all your heart. Never rely on what you think you know. Remember the LORD in everything you do, and he will show you the right way.*

PROVERBS 3:5–6 GNT

---

Would you even think about making a road trip without your GPS. . .or at least an old-fashioned map? Probably not. So what makes us think that we can go through life, the only life we get, without a road map? Yet many of us do that. What a tragedy!

God and His Word are our road maps. He says to trust Him completely. We can't rely on our own opinions and feelings. We must rely on Him, and He will direct us. We must get to know Him intimately through His Word and prayer. Then He will lead us in the right ways to go. We can put our hope and faith in Him to take us in the perfect direction for us.

Father, I put my trust in You as my guide.
Thank You for leading me. Amen.

# Pray and Boldly Believe

*"For this reason I tell you: When you pray and ask for something, believe that you have received it, and you will be given whatever you ask for."*

MARK 11:24 GNT

---

Is there some area in your life in which you need a change? Whatever the need may be, Jesus says to ask and boldly believe for it, be convinced that you will receive it, and it will be yours.

This is a hard scripture for many Christians to believe. Why don't we just take Jesus at His word? Either the Bible is true or it's not. We know it is true, so let's choose to believe that it means what it says. Let's stretch our faith and put our hope in God and His Word and see miracles in our lives.

This is a powerful scripture. Jesus Himself spoke it. Believe it!

Jesus, I choose to believe You and take you at Your word. Help me boldly believe you will answer my prayers. Amen.

# He Is Our Comforter

*He comforts us in all our troubles so that we can comfort others. When they are troubled, we will be able to give them the same comfort God has given us.*

2 CORINTHIANS 1:4 NLT

---

We live in a fallen world. Sometimes life is difficult. But God is our comforter, and He is always there for us. In this same way, we can comfort others.

Maybe you know someone who is going through a hard time right now. You can help lift that person by reaching out to them and sharing how God helped you through the same thing or something similar. In this way, you will help build their faith. You will be a minister from God to them.

You don't have to be a pastor or evangelist. Just be yourself. Show them love and listen to them if they need to pour their heart out to someone. Love them and then pray for them. You will be a life changer.

**Father, use me to be a giver of hope to someone today. Amen.**

# Give Thanks in All Things

*Be thankful in all circumstances, for this is God's will for you who belong to Christ Jesus.*

1 THESSALONIANS 5:18 NLT

---

One way to remain hopeful is to always give thanks in all circumstances. Let me be clear: this does not mean to thank God *for* all your circumstances. But it does mean to be thankful *in* all circumstances.

It's not that the Lord expects us to thank Him for being sick, broke, or sad. But He does expect us to be thankful while going through these things. By having an attitude of gratitude, we stay positive and lifted up in the Lord, focusing on His promises instead of our problems. Remember that this, too, shall pass. God is faithful and will always provide what we need when we need it. It may seem to us like He's running a bit late, but He is not.

**Thank You, Lord, for helping me to remain hopeful by having an attitude of gratitude in the midst of my less than desirable circumstances. Amen.**

# His Love Never Ends

*The faithful love of the LORD never ends! His mercies
never cease. Great is his faithfulness; his mercies begin
afresh each morning. I say to myself, "The LORD is
my inheritance; therefore, I will hope in him!"*

LAMENTATIONS 3:22–24 NLT

---

No matter what your situation is today, take heart, my
friend. The Lord is faithful, and His love never ends. His
mercies begin afresh each morning. Think about it. Every
day we can start again.

We may have messed up yesterday, but we don't have
to rehash it. He forgives and lets us start all over again.
What a relief that is!

We don't always experience that kind of grace from
people. But we know that our heavenly Father is perfect
in His love. He forgives over and over again. We can hope
in Him. And that is a sure thing because His Word says so.
Stop and praise God for His love and mercies. Thank Him
for His faithfulness. He deserves all the praise.

**Loving Father, I am so grateful for Your mercies that
never cease and for Your faithful love to me. Amen.**

# Every Good Thing Comes from Him

*Whatever is good and perfect is a gift
coming down to us from God our Father,
who created all the lights in the heavens.*

JAMES 1:17 NLT

---

Every good and perfect thing that has come to us has been from God above. He is the God who created the heavens and the earth. His power is magnificent. He is the one and only true God. We can totally put our hope and faith in Him.

Expect great and wonderful things from Him, because that is His heart toward you. He loves you so much. Show Him how much you love Him by living your best life. Give back to Him by using your gifts and talents in your best way possible to show your love to Him. This will bring great satisfaction to you.

Life is good! God is great! Praise Him in the morning. Praise Him at noon. Praise Him at night. Praise Him always. He is worthy!

Loving heavenly Father, I praise You,
for You alone are worthy. Amen.

# Feel God's Peace

*Don't worry about anything; instead, pray about
everything. Tell God what you need, and thank him for
all he has done. Then you will experience God's peace,
which exceeds anything we can understand. His peace will
guard your hearts and minds as you live in Christ Jesus.*
PHILIPPIANS 4:6–7 NLT

How can we experience God's peace? First, stop worrying and start praying to Him. You can tell Him anything and everything. He already knows how you feel, so you may as well be honest with Him. By doing this, you will experience His peace. This peace that comes from our heavenly Father is beyond anything we can understand.

Then let His peace guard your heart and mind. When the enemy of your soul tries to steal that peace, guard your thoughts. Go back to that peaceful place. Be determined that nothing and no one will take it from you.

Lord Jesus, I will choose to not worry but instead
pray about everything. I will guard my heart and
mind and stay in peace. Thank You, Lord.

# Pray and Sing

*Are any of you suffering hardships? You should pray.*
*Are any of you happy? You should sing praises.*
JAMES 5:13 NLT

God gives us the answer to our problems in His Word. He wants to help us overcome our feelings of hopelessness. He says if we're suffering hardships, we should pray. And He also says if we're happy, we should sing praises. Mulling around in our problems is no way to live. Cry out to God and give Him your hardships. In doing this, peace comes, and we can feel the joy of the Lord. Then we sing praises to Him.

Maybe you can't sing that well. He doesn't care. He loves to hear you sing anyway. Singing will lift your spirits and help you stay happy. Music is a powerful thing. Turn on some praise and worship music. Sing along with it. You'll be amazed at how your feelings will change.

Lord, I choose to pray and sing Your praises.
Thank You for always lifting my spirits when I come
to You. You are so faithful and loving. Amen.

# Praise Him for Everything He Has Done

*Praise the LORD! Praise God in his Temple!*
*Praise his strength in heaven! Praise him for the mighty*
*things he has done. Praise his supreme greatness.*

PSALM 150:1–2 GNT

---

Are you feeling hopeless? Does your situation have you down? God gives us the answer in His Word. He says to praise Him. He has given us instructions to praise Him in the temple, which means your church. Praise Him for His mighty power. For all the mighty things He has done. For His supreme greatness as the one true God.

If we focus on the magnificence of God instead of our troubles, our troubles begin to shrink in our minds. So lift up His name today. Thank Him for all the answers to prayer in the past. Encourage your heart in the Lord.

**Father, I choose to focus on Your greatness and Your faithfulness to always hear my prayers. You have proven to be faithful to me every time. So this time I am choosing to trust You again. In Jesus' name, amen.**

# *He Always Forgives*

*Create in me a clean heart, O God.*
*Renew a loyal spirit within me.*
PSALM 51:10 NLT

---

Perhaps you feel hopeless today because you have fallen back into sin. You messed up again. In your mind you're thinking, *How many times have I done this?*

In the Psalms, David had experienced this same thing. But he showed us what to do: he called out to God, asking Him to create in him a clean heart and renew his spirit. That's all we need to do too. And God is there every time to forgive and renew our spirit.

Aren't you glad for a forgiving heavenly Father? He will never give up on us. He forgives over and over again. His goodness and mercies never end.

Father, please forgive me again for my failures. I'm sorry. Increase my ability to stand strong in these times of trial. Help me to always come to You for strength before I mess up. I choose to follow Your ways, Lord. Amen.

# Filled with Joy

*We also pray that you will be strengthened with all his glorious power so you will have all the endurance and patience you need. May you be filled with joy, always thanking the Father.*

COLOSSIANS 1:11–12 NLT

The apostle Paul wrote to the Colossians that he was praying for them to be strengthened with God's glorious power so they would have all the endurance and patience they needed. He prayed they would be filled with joy and always be giving thanks to the Father. What a beautiful prayer. We can make that our prayer as well.

Through Jesus' death, burial, and resurrection, we have been delivered from the curse of sin. Because Jesus overcame death, hell, and the grave, we have victory through Him. What a glorious hope!

May God help us to live in all the power that He has given us.

Lord Jesus, help me to always live in the power of the resurrection. And may I always be filled with joy, giving thanks to You for Your work on the cross. Amen.

# His Unfailing Love

*"Understand, therefore, that the LORD your God is indeed God. He is the faithful God who keeps his covenant for a thousand generations and lavishes his unfailing love on those who love him and obey his commands."*

DEUTERONOMY 7:9 NLT

---

Our God is the only true God. He is faithful. He always keeps His covenant, and He lavishes His unfailing love on those who love and obey Him.

Can you see that picture in your mind's eye? Our heavenly Father lavishing His love on you? What would that look like? Imagine it. What a beautiful sight!

Not only does He lavish His love on you, but His love is unfailing. Why should you be discouraged? Focus on His ability, not your own. Think about His feelings and thoughts toward you, not your own feelings and thoughts about yourself. This is how you can renew your mind. Meditate on God's Word and His promises.

**Thank You, Father, that I can depend on Your unfailing love lavished on me. I love You, Jesus.**

# He Is Always with You

*"So be strong and courageous! Do not be afraid and do not panic before them. For the LORD your God will personally go ahead of you. He will neither fail you nor abandon you."*

DEUTERONOMY 31:6 NLT

---

Here's a verse for you today if you need hope. Joshua was facing a battle. But God's Word for him was to be strong and courageous. Do not be afraid. Do not panic. The Lord would go before him and would not fail or abandon him.

This is the heart of our heavenly Father. He feels the same about you. So whatever you're facing today, be strong and courageous. Do not panic in fear. Your heavenly Father will personally go ahead of you. He has promised to never fail you or abandon you. Believe it. It's the truth. It's the Word of God.

Father, You know the situations in my life. You know my human feelings and frailties. But I choose to trust You today, knowing that You will go ahead of me and work out everything. You promised to never fail or abandon me. I trust You completely today.

63

# Hold on Tightly

*Let us hold tightly without wavering to the hope we affirm, for God can be trusted to keep his promise.*

HEBREWS 10:23 NLT

---

If we really search the scriptures, we find that, again and again, the Lord encourages us to hold tightly to hope. Why? Because He has promised that He can be trusted to keep His promise. The more we read and meditate on His Word, the more we will believe it. This is how we renew our minds.

Do you tend to stay busy, trying to keep your mind off your troubles? When you finally sit down and get still, those troubles are still going to be there. The way we overcome is not by ignoring them but by changing our thinking. We meditate on His promises and get those beautiful words deeply planted in our hearts. Then when the next situation arises, the promises of God will be what comes to mind.

Father, help me to get Your Word deeply settled
in my heart so I'm prepared for all life's situations.
I want to be strong in hope and faith. Amen.

# *What Good News*

*"Don't be afraid, for I am with you. Don't be discouraged,
for I am your God. I will strengthen you and help you.
I will hold you up with my victorious right hand."*
ISAIAH 41:10 NLT

---

What good news! You are not alone. You don't have to
do life by yourself. God said He is your God. He is with
you. Don't be afraid, because He promised to strengthen
and help you. And even better news, He's holding you up.
Wow! Make sure you let that sink in—God is holding you!

You may feel alone, but you're not. Let that truth settle
in your heart. Meditate on it. Feel it. God is the Creator
of the universe, yet He is holding you. What's keeping you
from fulfilling your calling in life? Go for it! God is with you.

Father God, I praise You and thank You for
holding me in Your hands. You go before me
and with me. Why should I be afraid? I refuse
to be afraid. I trust You completely. Amen.

# He Is Constant

*I can never escape from your Spirit! I can never get away from your presence! If I go up to heaven, you are there; if I go down to the grave, you are there. If I ride the wings of the morning, if I dwell by the farthest oceans, even there your hand will guide me, and your strength will support me.*

PSALM 139:7–10 NLT

---

God is a never-failing, constant help to you. No matter where you go, no matter what you're going through, He is there. You are never alone.

Pour out your heart to Him. Talk to Him. He hears. He answers. You need never fear or feel alone. He is your best friend. He is better than anyone else, because He knows you best. He made you. He loves you. He's your heavenly Father.

> Dear heavenly Father, thank You that I can trust You to always be with me. You will never leave me alone. You give comfort and help right when I need it. I worship You. Amen.

# *He Always Forgives*

*But if we confess our sins to God, he will keep his*
*promise and do what is right: he will forgive us our*
*sins and purify us from all our wrongdoing.*

1 JOHN 1:9 GNT

---

If you have sinned, maybe you feel like God has left you. Never for a moment let that thought stay in your mind. He is always there, willing and ready to forgive you. Just confess your sin to Him, and you will be forgiven.

You don't have to beg Him. He is already willing. He still loves you. He never stopped loving you. He understands your weaknesses and wants to give you strength to overcome.

So what's holding you back? Do it now. Be restored to your heavenly Father. He's waiting.

**Father God, I'm sorry for my sin. I ask for Your forgiveness. Cleanse my heart and give me the strength to overcome this area of weakness in me. Thank You for always loving me. In Jesus' name, amen.**

# *You Belong to God*

*But you belong to God, my dear children. You have already
won a victory over those people, because the Spirit who lives
in you is greater than the spirit who lives in the world.*

1 JOHN 4:4 NLT

---

You are God's child. His Spirit lives in you, and His Spirit is greater than the spirit in the world. So with the Holy Spirit's aid, you can be and you are an overcomer! No matter what storms may come, you have everything you need to get through them. What a glorious hope and promise!

See yourself as an overcomer. Tell yourself you're an overcomer. God's Spirit lives in you and gives you the power. Let that truth resonate in your heart and mind. Believe it.

God has given you everything you need through Christ. He has already overcome this world. He is our victor. And through Him, you too can be victorious. Praise God!

Father, I have everything I need to be victorious
and overcome, because I belong to You!
You are my helper—always! Thank You!

# We Have Everything We Need

*By his divine power, God has given us everything we need for living a godly life. We have received all of this by coming to know him, the one who called us to himself by means of his marvelous glory and excellence.*

2 PETER 1:3 NLT

Because we are God's children, born of His Spirit through salvation, we have everything we need to live godly lives. Maybe you feel like a failure today. Or perhaps you are struggling with some feelings of lack. All of us are human and imperfect. However, we have this power given to us by God to enable us to live this life in a godly manner.

We certainly don't get perfectly godly overnight. Godliness is a process. But as we go to God and let Him work in our hearts, we can get better. We can learn to walk in the Spirit and overcome, even though we live in these earthly bodies.

Father God, I ask You to help me remember to come to You when I feel weak and let You change me by Your Holy Spirit. I want to be godly in my walk here on earth. Amen.

# He Will Be
# Your Guide

*Trust in the LORD with all your heart; do not depend
on your own understanding. Seek his will in all you
do, and he will show you which path to take.*

---

Over and over again in the Bible we see that God has
promised to show us which path to take. If we trust Him,
if we don't depend on our own understanding, and if
we seek His will in everything, He will show us the way.
Too often we forget to do this. Something happens, and
immediately we start to fret and worry.

But if we can learn to stop before that happens and
go to God for direction, our lives will be so much better.
God tells us repeatedly what to do to make life better. We
must remember to ask Him for His leadership rather than
trying things on our own without asking for His guidance.

However, if we do mess up, we know He still forgives
us and will be there to lead and guide anyway. He's so
patient and loving.

**Father, I am so very grateful for Your patience with me.**

# I Can Do This

*I can do all things through Christ which strengtheneth me.*
PHILIPPIANS 4:13 KJV

---

Most of us already know this scripture, but do we really believe it? How many times have we quoted it, only to add, "But. . ." There is no "but" after this verse, though. Either it's true or it's not. And we know it is true because it's God's Word.

Whatever God has called you to do, with His strength you can do it—and not just sort of good but excellently. He wouldn't call you to something only to embarrass you. He believes in you. He knows your ability. He made you. So that thing He's calling you to do, go do it! And do it excellently. Study. Practice. Learn. Do your best. Succeed. God wouldn't want anything less from you.

Father, I will move forward in my calling. I will quit
rationalizing and making excuses. I will do my best.
It will be my love offering to You, with thanksgiving for
this opportunity to fulfill my calling in life. Amen.

# Don't Think like the World

*Don't copy the behavior and customs of this world,
but let God transform you into a new person by changing
the way you think. Then you will learn to know God's
will for you, which is good and pleasing and perfect.*

ROMANS 12:2 NLT

---

In order to have a good life, we must not follow the world. However, we do live in this world. Some people have taken this scripture and gone to extremes and become very odd, and as the saying goes, "They are so heavenly minded they are no earthly good." That is not what God is meaning here in the verse. He wants to help us change the way we think. In doing this, we will learn what God's will is. And He even says that His will is good and pleasing and perfect.

We have to learn to live in this world in such a way that we can still be effective yet stand out attractively in the world. We want to draw people to Christ, not turn them away with our weirdness.

Lord, help me to be like You in every way. Amen.

# He Will Complete the Work in You

*And I am certain that God, who began the good work within you, will continue his work until it is finally finished on the day when Christ Jesus returns.*

PHILIPPIANS 1:6 NLT

---

Sometimes you might feel like some things never change. It's easy to become discouraged. But God has promised to complete the work He began in you. Don't give up. Keep moving forward in the right direction. In the daily grind it's hard to see progress. But little by little, progress is made. It's in the consistency of good habits.

Daily read your Bible and pray. Establish these habits just like you do other things in your life. The benefits will follow. God is not finished with you yet. He will complete the work in you. Believe that every day you're getting better and better.

Father God, thank You for not giving up on me.
Even when I feel I'm not making progress,
I will choose to keep doing the next right thing,
knowing You're still working on me. Amen.

# In His Presence Is Joy

*You will show me the way of life, granting me the joy of
your presence and the pleasures of living with you forever.*

PSALM 16:11 NLT

---

God says He will show us the way of life. Not only that,
but He will grant us the joy of being with Him and the
pleasures of living with Him forever—not only in eternity
but here in the world.

He takes delight in us and loves to see us happy. And
it is in His presence where we find true happiness. This
world will give us heartache. But He gives everlasting joy
and happiness.

What's not to like about that? Nothing.

Father God, show me Your ways. Grant me the
joy of Your presence and the pleasures of living
with You. Daily I choose to delight in Your ways.
I will meet with You daily and spend time with You,
so that I can truly know Your heart. For it's in Your
presence that I find happiness and peace. Amen.

# True Happiness and Joy

*The Lord is my strength and shield. I trust him with all my heart. He helps me, and my heart is filled with joy. I burst out in songs of thanksgiving.*

PSALM 28:7 NLT

---

The psalmist, David, had his own share of struggles with depression and discouragement. But he always came back around to praising God and lifting himself out of the doldrums. He found out that God was always there to help him.

Even after such low times, David would proclaim that his heart was filled with joy and he would burst out in songs of thanksgiving.

What an example he is to us! God made sure that David's struggles were recorded in scripture so that we would not feel alone and so that we would have a good example of what to do in dark times.

**Thank You, Father, for giving us Your Word to show us the way to overcome our times of feeling down. I choose to be like David and sing Your praises and trust You with all my heart. Amen.**

# Exalt the Lord

*Be still, and know that I am God: I will be exalted*
*among the heathen, I will be exalted in the earth.*
PSALM 46:10 KJV

---

Sometimes life gets crazy. Our schedules are hectic, and we feel frantically busy. It's times like these that we need to be still and know that He is God. Without that quiet time with the Lord each day, life tends to spiral out of control.

The fact that you're reading this devotional book shows you want to spend time with the Lord. Good for you. Be sure to be in the moment and not just check it off your list. If you're a list maker, checking things off your list feels good—but not as good as spending quality time with Jesus.

Be sure to shut down anything that could be a distraction so you can really get in His presence. It will be worth it. Be still and listen for His sweet voice.

Father, I choose to quiet my spirit and listen to
Your sweet voice. I will exalt You today. Amen.

# Seek Him First

*But seek ye first the kingdom of God, and His righteousness;*
*and all these things shall be added unto you.*

MATTHEW 6:33 KJV

God promises to take care of us. However, He also says to seek Him first. He has to be priority. Not in a legalistic way, but if we truly love Him, we will want to make Him a priority.

Set aside some time each day to read His Word and pray. Establishing this habit brings so many benefits. If we don't spend this time with Him on a regular basis, our lives can spiral out of control. And we can begin to feel frazzled, hopeless, and without purpose. This is no way to live life. God really does know what we need. There's a reason why He gives us His Word.

> Father, I choose to spend quality time with You daily. Thank You for coming to meet with me in these times. You give me so much hope. Amen.

# Don't Borrow Trouble from Tomorrow

*"So don't worry about tomorrow, for tomorrow will bring its own worries. Today's trouble is enough for today."*
MATTHEW 6:34 NLT

---

Jesus says not to worry about tomorrow because tomorrow will have its own troubles. Let's handle one day at a time.

Actually, what should we do about these situations anyway? Should we try to take control of them ourselves? Absolutely not. We should do our best to stay worry-free and trust God to take care of these situations in our lives. Often what we worry about never happens anyway. So our worrying is a total waste of time.

Keep your faith, trust, and hope in God your Father. He knows about tomorrow. He's already there.

Thank You, heavenly Father, that I can totally
trust You with my tomorrows. I rest in You
today. I'm choosing to remain in faith and hope
in You. You keep Your promises. Amen.

# Hope in the Lord

*"But blessed are those who trust in the LORD and
have made the LORD their hope and confidence."*
JEREMIAH 17:7 NLT

When we choose to trust in our heavenly Father and have
hope and confidence in Him, He says we will be blessed.
In the Bible, the word *blessed* means "happy," "favored," or
"satisfied." Don't you love those words? Who doesn't want
to be happy, favored, and satisfied?

Many times our heavenly Father shows His heart
toward us. When we put our hope and trust in God, He
will take care of us. He has good plans. This is great news!
Who wouldn't want to follow a heavenly Father who loves
us so much?

Keep your hope in Him. Be confident in the fact that
He has only good plans for you. And don't forget that whatever
life brings you, He will be there to get you through it.

**Thank You, Father, that You always get me through
difficult situations. I will keep my hope in You. Amen.**

# Blessed and Secured

*"They are like trees planted along a riverbank, with roots that reach deep into the water. Such trees are not bothered by the heat or worried by long months of drought. Their leaves stay green, and they never stop producing fruit."*

JEREMIAH 17:8 NLT

---

In this verse, those who trust in the Lord are being compared to trees planted along the river with roots going deep down into the water. Those trees are never bothered by the heat or drought. It says their leaves stay green, and they never stop producing fruit.

So it's best for us to be planted in God's Word, staying close to Him, and He will make sure we have everything we need. This is so comforting and assuring.

Let's get to know our heavenly Father. And how do we do that? By reading His Word, giving Him all our fears, and not only talking to Him but taking the time to actually listen for His voice. He will speak to us.

Father, I choose to plant myself firmly in You so the storms of life don't knock me down. Amen.

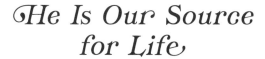

# He Is Our Source for Life

*"Yes, I am the vine; you are the branches. Those who remain in me, and I in them, will produce much fruit. For apart from me you can do nothing."*
JOHN 15:5 NLT

---

Jesus shows us how important it is to stay close to Him. He is the vine, and we are the branches. When we stay close to Him, He will help us to produce much fruit. In other words, when we stay close to Him, our lives will be meaningful and filled with purpose.

He also says that without Him we can do nothing. He is the one who gives us the energy, the strength, the purpose, and the knowledge of how to do what He calls us to do. Unless we stay close to Him, things won't go as well.

He created us and the world. He is our complete source for life.

**Thank You, Lord, for being my source. I will choose to stay close to You and let You show me the way to go. Amen.**

# He Is My Source for Hope

*I pray that God, the source of hope, will fill you completely with joy and peace because you trust in him. Then you will overflow with confident hope through the power of the Holy Spirit.*

ROMANS 15:13 NLT

---

If you feel without hope today, let this beautiful scripture encourage you. Go to God. He is your source of hope. He'll fill you completely with joy and peace when you trust in Him. Then you will abound in confident hope, which comes through the power of the Holy Spirit.

Who doesn't want confident hope? Who doesn't want joy and peace? He is the source of all of that. Pour your heart out to Him today. Tell Him everything. He knows anyway. And He understands you better than anyone else.

Then take the time to listen to what He has to say. Keep a journal and write down your thoughts. In doing that, you will see where He speaks to you.

**Father, thank You for speaking to me and being my source of hope. Amen.**

# The Hopes of the Godly

*The hopes of the godly result in happiness, but the expectations of the wicked come to nothing.*

PROVERBS 10:28 NLT

---

It matters *who* your hope and expectations are in. The godly put their hope and expectations in the one true God. That's why their result is happiness. However, the wicked person's expectations result in nothing. Why? They are hoping in the wrong thing/person. Initially the wicked may appear to get everything they want. But in the end, their lives will come crashing in around them.

This is why it is so very important to trust God. And sometimes this way of doing things may seem all messed up. But we know from God's Word that in the end, the believer wins.

And actually we can take nothing with us into eternity anyway. Only the things with eternal value matter.

Lord, help me to keep my focus on the right things—the things of God. That's really all that matters in the end. Amen.

# He Is Our Only Hope

*My soul, wait thou only upon God;*
*for my expectation is from him.*

PSALM 62:5 KJV

Maybe you're waiting for some things to change in your life. Again and again you have been disappointed. You've almost lost hope.

In whom or what have you been putting your hope? Maybe a spouse or a friend? Maybe your boss or your parents?

The psalmist David says that we should wait only upon God. People will fail us. People will always disappoint. But God never will. It may seem like He is not getting around to answering us. But we have to tell ourselves it's in His timing.

In the meantime, we continue to put our hope and expectation in Him. Thank Him in faith ahead of time for what He's doing. We know He is always working on our behalf.

**Father God, You are always working on my behalf. You are my only hope. Thank You! I trust in You alone. Amen.**

# Their Hope Was in Jesus to Calm the Storm

*And he arose, and rebuked the wind, and said
unto the sea, Peace, be still. And the wind
ceased, and there was a great calm.*

MARK 4:39 KJV

---

When the disciples were out in the boat with Jesus, a great storm came, and they were very afraid. Jesus was asleep in the boat. They didn't feel like He even cared. How could He be asleep through that storm? They woke Him and asked if He even cared if they perished. They hoped Jesus would do something to help.

You can sense their panic. Sometimes we panic too. But Jesus didn't panic then, and He doesn't panic now. He just got up and spoke to the storm. And immediately the wind stopped, and there was a great calm.

He still does this today. He will calm your storm too.

**Thank You, Jesus, for calming all my storms
when I call on You. You're always available,
willing, and ready to help. I love You, Lord!**

# Evidence of Something Unseen

*To have faith is to be sure of the things we hope for, to be certain of the things we cannot see.*

HEBREWS 11:1 GNT

---

To hope for something obviously means we don't have it yet. We all know what it's like to wish for something and have to wait for it. It can seem like our faith is not working. Our thoughts easily turn negative, and we get discouraged.

But the Bible talks about the evidence of things we can't see. That sounds like an oxymoron. How can we have evidence of something we can't see? Faith takes us there.

So, have faith. Believe you'll receive. Be grateful in the waiting. Remember that God is working. Don't doubt it. Feel that outcome, send those negative thoughts away, and build your faith again and again. This is living by faith, for sure!

**Thank You, Lord, for faith to see what seems impossible. While I wait, I will praise You.**

# Hope Is Waiting for What Is Still Unseen

*For it was by hope that we were saved; but if we see what we hope for, then it is not really hope. For who of us hopes for something we see?*

ROMANS 8:24 GNT

We as human beings don't like to wait. We even stand in the kitchen at our microwave and tell it to hurry up, right? We have become so accustomed to having things right now.

However, quite often we are required to wait for things. We pray and hope that God does what we need immediately. He doesn't always work like that, though. He knows we can build character in the waiting.

But you might say, "I don't want to wait. I don't want to build my character!" That's understandable. But His ways are not always our ways. But they are the best ways.

**Heavenly Father, You are good, always good. So as I wait in hope for the answers to come, I trust You and love You.**

# It's for Our Good

*But if we hope for what we do not yet
have, we wait for it patiently.*
ROMANS 8:25 NIV

---

What? You might find yourself saying, "Lord, what were
You thinking saying that in Your Word we wait *patiently*?"

Waiting patiently is certainly not easy. But our heavenly
Father doesn't make us wait just to aggravate us. He's not
up there thinking, *Let's see how long they can stick this one out!*

The more we are convinced that He is good and always
good, it becomes easier to wait. We can know He's working everything out for our good. So choose to believe in
His goodness. He's not trying to be difficult. We can truly
put our hope and faith in our loving heavenly Father. His
timing is perfect.

> Lord, help me remember that You are for me,
> not against me. You're not trying to be difficult.
> You're working for my good. Thank You, Father.
> I choose to believe this. In Jesus' name, amen.

# You Were Created in His Image

*For whom he did foreknow, he also did predestinate
to be conformed to the image of his Son, that he
might be the firstborn among many brethren.*

ROMANS 8:29 KJV

---

As believers, we have a purpose. We have been created by God and made in His image. We have a purpose and an unshakable hope through this truth.

When Satan tries to tell you that you're nothing, you're a mistake, you're beyond hope, and all his other lies, you can stand up to him with this truth that you were created in the image of God's Son, Jesus! And you were created for a purpose and plan. Nothing will stop you. Absolutely nothing!

Remember Satan is a liar. He hates you. He wants to see you fail. But he can't win. If we stand firm in the hope we have in Christ Jesus, knowing we are created in His image, the enemy of your soul can't win.

**Heavenly Father, help me stay focused on
Your plan and purpose for my life.**

# The Hope of Heaven

*"He will wipe away every tear from their eyes, and death shall be no more, neither shall there be mourning, nor crying, nor pain anymore, for the former things have passed away."*

REVELATION 21:4 ESV

---

When a loved one dies, we mourn and grieve. But for believers, it is not the last time we will see them. We have the hope of heaven. There will be no more parting of ways, no more tears, no more death, no more pain. Doesn't that sound amazing?

We may hurt and be sorrowful, but we have such great hope! All of us have loved ones who have gone on before us. Just imagine seeing them again. Do you ever wonder what they are doing now? It's fun to dream of the possibilities, isn't it?

Revelation 21 goes on to say in the next verse that God is making everything new. We can't even begin to picture how awesome it will be!

Father, thank You that I can look forward
to the day I will see my loved ones again.
Thank You for the hope of heaven. Amen.

# Heaven Is Going to Be Wonderful

*"Don't let your hearts be troubled. Trust in God,
and trust also in me. There is more than enough room
in my Father's home. If this were not so, would I have
told you that I am going to prepare a place for you?"*

JOHN 14:1–2 NLT

---

Your soul is going to live forever. Death is not the end. Our heavenly Father is preparing a place for us in heaven. And Jesus said when it's ready, He would come for us.

Regardless of the situation we may live in here in this fallen world, our future is bright. We have a blessed hope of eternity with Jesus in heaven. And it won't be boring. We won't be sitting on the banks of the river just dangling our feet. We will have so many wonderful things to do. This is our glorious hope!

Father, I praise You for the glorious hope of heaven.
I thank You that Jesus is getting a place ready for me, and
He will come and get me when that time comes. Amen.

# A Better Day Is Coming

*But we are citizens of heaven, where the Lord Jesus Christ lives. And we are eagerly waiting for him to return as our Savior. He will take our weak mortal bodies and change them into glorious bodies like his own, using the same power with which he will bring everything under His control.*

PHILIPPIANS 3:20–21 NLT

---

We are not of this world. We are spiritual beings with an eternal future. We will get a new body, a glorious one just like Jesus' body. How exciting!

We can rest assured that our future is bright. God is a good Father, and He has great plans for our future, both here on this earth and for eternity. No mind can fathom and no eye has seen (1 Corinthians 2:9). What a day it will be when we see Jesus!

When this life is over, we have only just begun!

Jesus, I eagerly wait for Your return. I long to see You and my loved ones who are already there. Oh, what a blessed hope!

# Looking Forward in Hope

*For this world is not our permanent home;*
*we are looking forward to our home yet to come.*
HEBREWS 13:14 NLT

---

If you're discouraged today about your future, don't be disheartened. Over and over in scripture we see that God is good and has good plans for our future. He has great things for us—not only now but in heaven forever as well.

He's preparing our home. And we can be sure that it will be better than any home we have ever lived in here on this earth. And He knows us so well that our new homes will be exactly like we would like them. There is a great surprise coming. How about a beautiful home on the water or in the mountains? Dream about it. It will lift your emotions and bring you joy. We have lots of wonderful things to look forward to in our future.

**Father, please help me to keep my mind on the wonderful future in heaven with You and my loved ones. I cannot even conceive it! I am so excited and grateful! Amen.**

# We Have an Inheritance

*And we have a priceless inheritance—an inheritance that is kept in heaven for you, pure and undefiled, beyond the reach of change and decay.*

1 PETER 1:4 NLT

---

If you don't have much to call your own in this world, a better day is coming. We have an inheritance in heaven—a priceless one! Sounds pretty amazing, doesn't it? God is keeping it in heaven for us so that it will be pure and undefiled, where it cannot change or decay.

Don't you just love this? Again and again we see that our heavenly Father is taking care of us, here as well as in our future in heaven.

Spend some time imagining what this might be. And when you've used up your imagination, you haven't even begun to picture the greatness of it. The Bible says that no one can conceive it.

Father, thank You that You have an inheritance stored up for me in heaven. Thank You for Jesus as my Savior. I love You, and I'm grateful! Amen.

# Our Anchor of Hope

*On our behalf Jesus has gone in there before*
*us and has become a high priest forever,*
*in the priestly order of Melchizedek.*

HEBREWS 6:20 GNT

---

We have an unbreakable and unshakable anchor holding
our souls to God. What a beautiful thought! Our anchor
of hope is at the throne of God in heaven, where Jesus is.
And He is interceding for us there.

Whatever you may be going through today, Jesus is
interceding for you. He is in heaven with God the Father,
telling Him all about your situation. He loves you so much.
And He knows all your needs. Give your burdens to the
Lord and leave them there. Tell Him everything. He's waiting for you to talk to Him. He loves to commune with you.

Jesus, I leave my burdens in Your care today.
You know all about them. You are at work even
when I don't see it. You are interceding for
me. I trust You! Thank You, Lord! Amen.

# Hope Is Never Lost

*We were given this hope when we were saved. (If we already have something, we don't need to hope for it. But if we look forward to something we don't yet have, we must wait patiently and confidently.)*

ROMANS 8:24–25 NLT

---

Hope indicates that we are waiting for something that has not happened yet. When we believed Jesus for our salvation, we could not actually see that happening in the physical. But we believe it in our hearts and know that spiritually we are changed.

Likewise in other areas of our lives, we hope for what has not yet happened. But if you firmly believe that God has promised to fulfill every need you have, you can rest and be assured and stand firm in your hope and faith that it will happen. He never fails.

Hope is never lost! We keep waiting for it to be fulfilled. That's truly living by faith.

**Father God, help me when my hope and faith are weak. Enable me to stay strong in You. In Jesus' name, amen.**

# Be Confident in Hope

*Now faith is the substance of things hoped
for, the evidence of things not seen.*
HEBREWS 11:1 KJV

---

Believing in God and His character, knowing His heart
toward you is good, trusting that He's always faithful and
will never fail you. . .this kind of faith brings hope into
reality.

So if you find yourself with little hope, spend more
time in God's Word to increase your understanding of
God and His character. When you become immovable in
your knowledge of God's goodness, His love, His mercy,
His kindness toward you, then you grow stronger in faith.
And faith brings our hopes into reality. That's when we
will see our prayers answered. And even if you have to
wait a little while on God's timing, don't waver. Keep on
trusting that He's at work.

Father, thank You that I can be confident in hope.
I will work on building and strengthening my faith.
I trust You completely, Father. In Jesus' name, amen.

# You Can Be Strong

*Then Christ will make his home in your hearts
as you trust in him. Your roots will grow down
into God's love and keep you strong.*

EPHESIANS 3:17 NLT

---

You don't have to be weak. You can be strong. This is because Christ made His home in your heart when you trusted Him as your Savior. This enables you to be rooted and grounded in love. Because Christ lives in you, you can walk in love. He will give you the power to respond in love to those around you—even those who may be a little unlovable.

In our human nature, this is difficult. But with Christ making His home in our hearts, we have His love in us, enabling us to be loving to others. This is how we can help win the world to Christ. They need us to show them the love of God.

**Father, help me to walk in love. I want to show
others the love of Christ. In Jesus' name, amen.**

# Hope Is a Gift from Our Heavenly Father

*And this hope will not lead to disappointment. For we know how dearly God loves us, because he has given us the Holy Spirit to fill our hearts with his love.*

ROMANS 5:5 NLT

---

The ability to have hope is a gift from our heavenly Father. He gave us His Holy Spirit to be our helper and comforter. And the Holy Spirit fills our hearts with His love. Without God's hope and love, we are lost.

Since hope is a gift from your heavenly Father, be sure to not discount it by letting your thoughts run wild with worry and fear. It's always better to be hopeful and at peace.

Hopelessness is an awful feeling. You don't want to go there. Perhaps you are there right now? You don't have to stay there. Decide to change your thinking. Call out to God and ask Him to bring back your hope and increase your faith.

**Father, I ask You to help me accept this gift of hope from You. May I never squander it. Amen.**

# Hope Endures Forever

*Don't envy sinners, but always continue to
fear the Lord. You will be rewarded for this;
your hope will not be disappointed.*

PROVERBS 23:17–18 NLT

---

Sometimes our friends who are unbelievers seem to have it better than we do. That's frustrating. However this scripture says that if we continue to fear the Lord, we will be rewarded and our hope will not be disappointed.

"Fear the Lord" means to have awe and respect for Him. It doesn't mean to be afraid of Him. How could we have a close and loving relationship with God if we were afraid of Him? That's not possible.

So draw close to God. Get to know Him and let Him be your everything. Then your hope will last forever. Don't envy sinners. Their day is coming.

Father, I choose to not let it bother me when I see others prosper more than me. I will make a choice to get closer to You. And in doing this, You will take care of me. I don't need to worry. Amen.

# There Are Benefits from Trusting God

*But those who trust in the LORD will find new strength.*
*They will soar high on wings like eagles. They will run*
*and not grow weary. They will walk and not faint.*

ISAIAH 40:31 NLT

There are definite benefits from trusting in the Lord. We will find new strength. We will soar high like eagles. We will run and not get tired. We will walk and not faint. Who doesn't want those benefits?

Maybe trusting in the Lord will help us stay young. We all would like that, wouldn't we? We can't guarantee it, but we can know that trusting in the Lord instead of worrying about everything might keep a few wrinkles away from our faces. All that good, clean living is worth something, right?

This scripture is a good one to lean on for energy and overcoming difficulties. Trusting God is always a winner!

Lord, I choose to trust You. Thank You that because I do that, I will have new strength and energy. Amen.

# Fix Your Hope on Grace

*Therefore, preparing your minds for action, and being sober-minded, set your hope fully on the grace that will be brought to you at the revelation of Jesus Christ.*

1 PETER 1:13 ESV

The Lord wants us to keep our hearts and minds ready for what life may bring. It's so important to keep good track of our thoughts and put them in the right places. We need to stay alert and fix our hope, our earnest expectations, on marvelous grace.

This grace is coming to you. We have the power to change through Jesus Christ. We don't have to settle for a mediocre life. In fact, we had better not! God delights in our doing the best we can to overcome and flourish. He likes to see us succeed and be fulfilled in life. Set your goals and go out and make them happen.

Father, I will do my best with the talents and gifts You have given me. Thank You for trusting me with these gifts. I give You the praise and glory. Amen.

# Don't Give Up

*Rejoice in hope, be patient in tribulation,*
*be constant in prayer.*
ROMANS 12:12 ESV

Sometimes we may have to "work at" having hope. In the natural we don't feel it. But if we put forth the actions, the feelings will follow, and we will have continual joy.

We can't give up when trouble comes; we must be patient in our trials. We might not love that instruction, but it's for our good.

So, keep talking to God all the time. He knows what you're going through. He knows your personality. He made you. He knows exactly what you need and when you need it.

He is your source for hope, comfort, peace, and fulfillment. No matter what your circumstances are, you can have joy in your heart from communing with God.

So rejoice in hope. This too shall pass. A better day is coming. Believe it.

**Lord Jesus, help me to rejoice in hope, be patient, and pray continually. I want to be like You. Amen.**

# Hope of Glory

*To them God chose to make known how great among
the Gentiles are the riches of the glory of this mystery,
which is Christ in you, the hope of glory.*

COLOSSIANS 1:27 ESV

---

We have this wonderful hope of glory as believers.
Because we have trusted Christ as Lord and Savior, we
know we will be eternally with our heavenly Father in
heaven when we die.

At salvation, we are positioned *in* Christ and seated
*with* Christ. He gives us His life. We were given the righteousness of Christ. Because of this, we have the power
to overcome sin, the devil, and our old sinful nature. We
receive absolutely everything we need to overcome in life.
The power that raised Christ from the dead lives in us.
If this is true—and it is—then there is absolutely nothing
we cannot conquer through His power that lives in us.
This is great news!

> Thank You, Father, for this great hope of
> glory. I praise You that I can overcome
> through Your power that lives in me.

# *He Will Keep You Strong*

*Now you have every spiritual gift you need as you eagerly wait for the return of our Lord Jesus Christ. He will keep you strong to the end so that you will be free from all blame on the day when our Lord Jesus Christ returns.*

1 CORINTHIANS 1:7–8 NLT

---

We have everything necessary to be able to live daily until Jesus Christ comes back to get us to take us home to heaven. He will also keep us strong so that we will be free from sin and blame.

So don't waste time and energy worrying about the future, since we have everything we need through Christ. And we can eagerly look forward to His return. Heaven is our eternal home. We will be with Jesus, all the saints who are already there, and our friends and family who believed in Jesus and have gone on before us.

**Thank You, Father, for keeping me strong and helping me to eagerly wait for Your return. Amen.**

# *Jesus Understands Our Weaknesses*

*This High Priest of ours understands our weaknesses, for he faced all of the same testings we do, yet he did not sin. So let us come boldly to the throne of our gracious God. There we will receive his mercy, and we will find grace to help us when we need it most.*

HEBREWS 4:15–16 NLT

Jesus understands our weaknesses because He went through every type of thing that we go through. He lived on earth as a human just like us, yet He did not sin.

So He invites us to come to Him boldly for grace and mercy when we need it. And we are guaranteed to find help when we need it. He is always available, always ready and able to help His children.

Go to Him today and find strength. He never fails.

Dear Lord, I'm so grateful that You understand all my shortcomings. Help me to constantly come to You in those times of need and let You be my helper. In Your name, amen.

# How Rich Are the Blessings

*I ask that your minds may be open to see his light, so that*
*you will know what is the hope to which he has called you,*
*how rich are the wonderful blessings he promises his people,*
*and how very great is his power at work in us who believe.*
EPHESIANS 1:18–19 GNT

---

There is something better about daylight than darkness if you struggle with thoughts of depression. Not that daylight is the cure-all, but it certainly helps.

If your mind is open to see God's light, you will know the hope to which He has called you. His blessings for you are wonderful and rich. His power is very great, working in you as a believer. See it. Believe it. This is wonderful news. Think on it. Meditate on God and His blessings for you. Things will certainly begin to look better and brighter.

Lord, help us to believe Your Word. We don't
want to discount anything You have planned for
us as Your children. In Jesus' name, amen.

# Anything Is Possible If You Believe

*"What do you mean, 'If I can'?" Jesus asked. "Anything is possible if a person believes."*

MARK 9:23 NLT

---

What are you believing for? Do you *really* believe? Can you see it happening in your future? Maybe you're praying for a wayward child or spouse. God knows your hurting heart. He cares, and He wants them to come back to Him too.

So since we know it's His will, we don't have to ask, wondering if He will really do this. But since this person has free will, we do need to pray that God will move on their heart, helping them desire Him again. We can ask the Lord to cause them to miss the presence of the Holy Spirit. We can ask that the things of this world look really cheap and worthless.

Father, I pray for my wayward loved ones today.
May their hearts be softened toward You,
and may they long for Your Holy Spirit's
presence in their lives. In Jesus' name, amen.

# Pray to God for Help

*They talk about me and say, "God will not help
him." But you, O LORD, are always my shield from
danger; you give me victory and restore my courage.
I call to the LORD for help, and from his sacred hill he
answers me. I lie down in sleep, and all night long the
LORD protects me. I am not afraid of the thousands
of enemies who surround me on every side.*

PSALM 3:2–6 GNT

In our fear, the best thing to do is call out to the Lord.
That's what the psalmist David did when he had extreme
reasons to fear—people were trying to kill him! Most of
us have never been in that situation.

David called to the Lord, and the Lord heard him.
Then David was able to lie down and sleep. And all night
long the Lord watched over him. The Lord even took his
fear away. He will do the same for you. Trust Him and
never be afraid.

Thank You, Father, for protecting me and
helping me to be at peace. Amen.

# He Will Redeem You

*But the LORD will redeem those who serve him.*
*No one who takes refuge in him will be condemned.*

PSALM 34:22 NLT

---

To be redeemed means that you have been saved or delivered from sin and its consequences. So, since we are redeemed, we should show our love to the Lord by serving Him and giving Him our whole lives.

If we take refuge in the Lord, we will not be condemned. We can have a guilt-free conscience. Oh, what peace and hope we have in Christ.

We have been freed from our sin, and we are no longer slaves to sin. If we take refuge in the Lord, He gives us grace to overcome our weaknesses. What a wonderful blessing to be redeemed and set free from condemnation!

> Father, I give You my life to honor You and
> show my love to You for all You have done
> for me. Thank You for accepting me and not
> condemning me. I praise Your name! Amen.

# His Protection Guarantee

*"When you pass through the waters, I will be with you; and through the rivers, they shall not overwhelm you; when you walk through fire you shall not be burned, and the flame shall not consume you."*

ISAIAH 43:2 ESV

---

God does not promise that we won't go through trials and difficulties. Life is not perfect. But He did promise protection through these things. He said even though we pass through the waters, we will not drown. And when we pass through the fire, the flame will not consume us.

Let's recall the story in the third chapter of Daniel, where the three Hebrew men were thrown into the furnace of fire. God sent a fourth man to protect them. When the king looked in and saw four men, not three, he couldn't believe it.

The Holy Spirit was there and protected them! And the Holy Spirit will walk through everything with you too.

**Father, today I choose to trust You to walk with me through every trial and difficulty that I face. In Jesus' name, amen.**

# He's the Lifter of Your Head

*But you, O LORD, are a shield about me,*
*my glory, and the lifter of my head.*

PSALM 3:3 ESV

---

David was so afraid and discouraged. People were looking for him to kill him. But he went to the Lord. He prayed this beautiful prayer. He was praising God for being his shield, his glory, and the lifter of his head.

Are you afraid and discouraged today? Let God be your protector. Let Him lift your head. Sometimes we may be so down that our body language even looks down. Our head may be down, our countenance sad.

But GOD! Let Him lift your head and encourage you today. He loves you so much. He will protect you. He wants to take care of you. You are His child. He is calling you today to come let Him cheer you up. So let Him do it.

**Father, I come to You with my heaviness and choose to let You lift my head and be my shield and my glory. In Jesus' name, amen.**

# I Choose No Fear

*I will not be afraid of many thousands of people*
*who have set themselves against me all around.*

PSALM 3:6 ESV

---

When David was running for his life with thousands of people after him, he had to be petrified! However, he spoke to the Lord and said, "I will not be afraid even though thousands of people have surrounded me to take my life. I will not be afraid; I will trust the Lord" (paraphrased).

Can we actually do that? We may not have thousands of people trying to kill us, but sometimes life feels like there are many things in our way or on our minds to take our peace. It's times like these that we have to choose not to be afraid of the situation. We have to stay at peace in our minds and trust our heavenly Father to work everything out for our good.

When we learn to actually do this, peace comes.

**Father, thank You for Your peace that comes from trusting You and not being afraid. Amen.**

# Put on Your New Self

*If then you have been raised with Christ, seek the
things that are above, where Christ is, seated at the
right hand of God. Set your minds on things that
are above, not on things that are on earth.*

COLOSSIANS 3:1–2 ESV

---

In this passage of scripture, the apostle Paul was instructing the Colossian people who had become followers of Christ to change their thinking. He told them to put their thoughts on godly things, the things of the Lord, not on the things of this earth.

God had this put in the scriptures for a reason. He knew that it's human nature to struggle with our thinking. It's not good to dwell on our past failures. We have been redeemed and changed. We are new creatures. Old things have passed away, and all things have become new.

Father, help me change my thinking. And may
I not be so prone to get down and negative
in my thoughts. In Jesus' name, amen.

# *But Until Then*

*For this light momentary affliction is preparing for us an eternal weight of glory beyond all comparison, as we look not to the things that are seen but to the things that are unseen. For the things that are seen are transient, but the things that are unseen are eternal.*

2 CORINTHIANS 4:17–18 ESV

While we are going through difficult situations, the Lord wants us to look beyond the circumstances to what we can benefit from them. Life brings trials, but God helps us grow and learn from these things. He works them all out for our good.

Beyond the actual situations we are in, there's a bigger picture. God wants to change us into better people and equip us for our future.

Until then, even if we don't know why we are enduring hard times, we rest in God. He has nothing but good plans for us. And He knows what is best.

Father, I trust You and Your bigger
plan and purpose for my life.

# *He Has Mercy*

*And he cried out, "Jesus, Son of David, have mercy on me!"*
LUKE 18:38 ESV

---

As Jesus came into the city of Jericho, a blind man was sitting by the roadside begging. He was desperate. He could hear all the noise and confusion, but he didn't know what was happening. He asked those around him, and they said Jesus of Nazareth was passing by.

The man cried out to Jesus, hoping He would have mercy on him. The people told him to hush. But he cried out even more.

Jesus stopped and asked for the man to be brought to Him. Then Jesus asked the man what he wanted. He said, "Lord, let me recover my sight."

Jesus said to him, "Recover your sight; your faith has made you well" (Luke 18:42 ESV). Immediately he could see!

This is the heart of our heavenly Father. He loves you!

**Lord, thank You for having mercy on me. Thank You for changing me into the person You created me to be. I surrender to Your perfect plan, Lord. Amen.**

# *Victory Is Ours*

*But thank God! He gives us victory over sin
and death through our Lord Jesus Christ.*

1 CORINTHIANS 15:57 NLT

That thing you're struggling with today, whatever it is, God wants to give you victory over it. Jesus came, died, and rose again, overcoming sin, hell, and the grave for *us*! He did this so we wouldn't have to continue struggling. That is good news!

Jesus conquered sin and the grave. So we don't have to feel defeated. We can have victory. And we don't have to fear death. Death for the believer is just a passing over into the other world. We are never alone.

So walk in your victory today! Rise above those other situations that tend to drag you down. Refuse to let them control you. God is walking right beside you, giving you the power to overcome.

**Father, thank You that You give me the power to overcome. Thank You for giving me victory over sin and death through Jesus, my Lord and Savior. Amen.**

# Work Happily

*So, my dear brothers and sisters, be strong and immovable.*
*Always work enthusiastically for the Lord, for you know*
*that nothing you do for the Lord is ever useless.*

1 CORINTHIANS 15:58 NLT

---

God doesn't waste anything. Nothing we do for Him is ever useless. So since we know Jesus overcame sin and the grave for us, let's be strong and immovable. Don't be tossed about emotionally with every little whim. Don't give in to empty emotions. Remind yourself what He did for you. Start thanking Him. Praise Him. Do life enthusiastically for the Lord. Be joyful.

You may not feel those feelings at first. But if you start by just doing, the feelings will follow simply from your act of obedience. He will reward you for your choice to just do the next right thing.

Lord, I choose to be joyful. I will put a praise on my
lips. I will thank You for all Your goodness to me.
I will recall all the things You have done for me in the
past. I will work happily as unto the Lord. Amen.

# God Is Looking Out for You

*Then Joshua said to his officers, "Don't be afraid or discouraged. Be determined and confident because this is what the LORD is going to do to all your enemies."*

JOSHUA 10:25 GNT

Joshua told his men to not be afraid or discouraged but to be determined and confident, because the Lord would take care of them. God is the same today. His nature has not changed. If He would do it for Joshua's men, He will certainly do it for us.

So what are you facing today? Don't be afraid or discouraged. Be determined and confident. Not in your own ability but in God's ability. He is the one giving you the strength and courage. He is the one who goes before you and prepares the way. All you have to do is follow Him. Take His hand and let Him lead you in the right direction.

Father, thank You for looking out for me and leading me in the right direction. I will not be afraid or discouraged. I trust You. Amen.

# Let's Do Our Part

*Jesus said to him, "Get up, pick up your mat,
and walk." Immediately the man got well;
he picked up his mat and started walking.*

JOHN 5:8–9 GNT

---

Jesus saw a man who had been sick for thirty-eight years.
So Jesus asked him if he wanted to get well. The man told
Jesus he didn't have anyone to lift him up and put him
into the pool. He even went on to say that every time he
tried to get in, somebody else got there first.

Do you sense a little attitude of feeling sorry for himself? Perhaps.

So, what did Jesus do next? He looked at the man and
told him to get up, pick up his mat, and walk. The man did,
and he was instantly healed. How amazing! It's interesting
too—Jesus told the man to do something first. Sometimes
we might have to take that first step of faith.

**Father, help me to be willing to take that first step
of faith. My strength comes from You. Amen.**

# Hope Because of the Resurrection

*Blessed be the God and Father of our Lord Jesus Christ! According to his great mercy, he has caused us to be born again to a living hope through the resurrection of Jesus Christ from the dead.*

1 PETER 1:3 ESV

Praise God for His great mercy. He has given us a living hope through the resurrection of Jesus Christ. He did this so that we might be born again and given life everlasting.

We really can't say it enough—what wonderful hope we have through Jesus' death, burial, and resurrection! He conquered sin, hell, and the grave for us. Death has no sting for the believer. And it's just a temporary separation for those of us left behind after a loved one who believed in Jesus dies. We will see them again. What a sweet consolation.

**Thank You, Lord, that You provide the great hope of the resurrection. Someday I will see my loved ones again. You are so good. Amen.**

# I Trust You, God

*When I am afraid, I put my trust in you.*
*In God, whose word I praise, in God I trust;*
*I shall not be afraid. What can flesh do to me?*

PSALM 56:3–4 ESV

---

Fear is a strong emotion. We all have it from time to time. But the more we send that fear away in Jesus' name and put our trust in God, our Father, the easier it will be. Faith works like a muscle. The more you use it, the stronger it gets.

So use your faith today. Refuse to entertain thoughts of fear, and start praising God. There is such tremendous power in praise. That is how we should be fighting our battles. Put on some praise and worship music. Sing along. Fight in faith.

Heavenly Father, I choose to fight in faith. I will not let fear control me. I will choose to praise You, worship You, and lift up Your name. Thank You, Father, that when I do that, great peace comes. In Jesus' name, amen.

# God Is My Salvation

*"Behold, God is my salvation; I will trust, and will not be afraid; for the LORD GOD is my strength and my song, and he has become my salvation."*

ISAIAH 12:2 ESV

When we read the Bible, we can find a lot of people who are just like us. Isaiah had to build up his faith too. We would do well to follow his lead.

In those times of weakness and fear, tell the Lord that He is your salvation. Tell Him you will trust and not be afraid. He is your strength. He gives you a song to sing. So take some time to praise Him.

It's good to proclaim these things to Him. Call on Him anytime. He's always listening.

Heavenly Father, I thank You that You're always listening for me to call on You. Thank You that You're helping me to live in faith and not fear. You are such a good Father. Amen.

# *Be Courageous*

*"Be strong and courageous, for you are the one who will lead these people to possess all the land I swore to their ancestors I would give them."*

JOSHUA 1:6 NLT

---

Here God was giving instructions to Joshua before going in to possess the land. Evidently Joshua was struggling a little with being afraid. Again we see another Bible character who was very human in that he also had fear and insecurities at times.

This is good for us to see because it helps us realize that the Bible characters weren't perfect either. They were human just like us. God had to give Joshua a little pep talk.

He sometimes has to give us a pep talk too. He wants us to be strong and courageous and trust Him to keep His Word. He never fails.

Thank You, Father, that You always keep Your word. I can count on You. Help me to be strong and courageous and to move forward in the plan You have for me. Show me Your plan for me daily, and I will walk in it. Amen.

# Hope for a Good Life

*"Study this Book of Instruction continually. Meditate on it day and night so you will be sure to obey everything written in it. Only then will you prosper and succeed in all you do."*

JOSHUA 1:8 NLT

---

If you're hoping to succeed in life, the only way to do that is to follow God's Word. If we know what His Word says and we obey it, then life will go well.

That's not to say that we won't have trials and hardships at times. But if we are putting God first in our lives, He will show us the way during those times as well. Everything we need for life and godliness is found in His Word. So be in His Word daily. This is your guide for life.

Father, thank You for showing me true wisdom through Your Word. I believe that Your plans for me are good and You will show me every step to take. I put my hope and faith in You today! Amen.

# The Lord Your God Is with You

*"This is my command—be strong and courageous!*
*Do not be afraid or discouraged. For the LORD*
*your God is with you wherever you go."*

JOSHUA 1:9 NLT

---

God commands us to be strong and courageous. We're not to be afraid or discouraged. This is not just a little suggestion. He didn't say, "Try not to worry or be afraid or discouraged." No! He said, "This is my command—be strong and courageous! Do not be afraid or discouraged."

Then He added, "The LORD your God is with you wherever you go." This is great news! He is always with us. He is always guiding us and showing us the way. He is faithful. We can definitely put our hope and trust in Him.

Lean on Him today. Let Him get you through every situation in your life. He is your constant companion.

Father, thank You for being with me at all times.
Thank You for giving me strength and courage. I choose to
trust You today and put my hope and faith in You. Amen.

# Put Your Hope and Trust in the Lord (Part 1)

*The LORD said to me, "I chose you before I gave you life, and before you were born I selected you to be a prophet to the nations." I answered, "Sovereign LORD, I don't know how to speak; I am too young." But the LORD said to me, "Do not say that you are too young, but go to the people I send you to, and tell them everything I command you to say. Do not be afraid of them, for I will be with you to protect you. I, the LORD, have spoken!"*

JEREMIAH 1:4–8 GNT

Jeremiah doubted his ability to do what God had commanded him. He felt he was too young and didn't know how to speak. Sometimes we do the same thing. We argue with God.

But God didn't let Jeremiah get away with that. He told him to not be afraid. Then He said, "I, the LORD, have spoken!" In other words, "Hush up, Jeremiah, and get going!"

Lord, help me quit analyzing and fearing
every little situation. Amen.

# Put Your Hope and Trust in the Lord (Part 2)

*"They will fight you, but they will fail. For I am with you, and I will take care of you. I, the LORD, have spoken!"*

JEREMIAH 1:19 NLT

---

Jeremiah is still carrying on the conversation with the Lord. Don't we do that at times? But God is being such a good heavenly Father and giving him comfort and peace about it. Over and over again, God tells Jeremiah that He will be with him and that He will take care of him. He assures him that the enemy will come and fight him, but they will fail. Why? Because "I am with you, and I will take care of you." And for emphasis, He adds, "I, the LORD, have spoken!"

In other words, it's a done deal. Move on and move forward. When God says something, He means it. We don't need to argue with Him. He knows all things, and we can trust Him.

**Father, thank You for helping me to move on and move forward with my life. Amen.**

# *Be Bold*

*For God has said, "I will never leave you; I will never abandon you." Let us be bold, then, and say, "The Lord is my helper, I will not be afraid. What can anyone do to me?"*

HEBREWS 13:5–6 GNT

Be bold and say aloud, "The Lord is my helper, I will not be afraid. What can anyone do to me?" Say it again and then again. Feel the words. Feel His assurance and love wash all over your spirit. His presence is real. He is a true comfort. A true companion. A loving heavenly Father who always keeps His word. Build your faith this way. The enemy of your soul won't have a chance!

> Father, thank You that I can boldly proclaim that You are my helper and I will not be afraid. I thank You that Your Holy Spirit is always with me, giving me comfort and peace. He brings me hope when things seem hopeless. I praise Your name! Amen.

# Keep Your Eyes on the Goal

*"Be strong and very courageous. Be careful to obey all the instructions Moses gave you. Do not deviate from them, turning either to the right or to the left. Then you will be successful in everything you do."*

JOSHUA 1:7 NLT

---

God told Joshua to be strong, courageous, and obedient. Obviously it was very important for Joshua to stay on the path and not deviate from it at all. God then said that if Joshua did this, he would be successful in everything he did.

Today, if we follow God's Word and His plan for our lives, He will reward us too. God knows exactly what we need to do. So obviously it would behoove us to listen and obey. How can we expect God to bless us if we willingly go against His instructions? So let's be firm in our commitment to God and obedience to Him.

Father, I choose to listen, follow, and obey You at all times. When I start to get off track, please pull me back. I want to follow You. Amen.

# You're Not Alone

*The temptations in your life are no different from what others experience. And God is faithful. He will not allow the temptation to be more than you can stand. When you are tempted, he will show you a way out so that you can endure.*

1 CORINTHIANS 10:13 NLT

---

Do you ever feel like you're the only one going through something? That's a trick of the devil. But remember he's a liar. God's Word says that your temptations are no different from what others experience. You're not alone. And God is faithful and will not let the situation last longer than you can stand. He will show you a way out if you go to Him for guidance.

Sometimes we go to a friend for help. And that's okay if we're careful to go to a friend who can be trusted. But the very best person to go to is Jesus. He knows you best. He has all the answers.

Father, You know what I'm going through now. Remind me that Your strength is made perfect in my weakness. I lean on You, Lord. Thank You for strength. Amen.

# Sweet Sleep Is Yours

*I lay down and slept; I woke again,*
*for the LORD sustained me.*
PSALM 3:5 ESV

---

The Lord will give you sweet sleep when you need it. While David was running from his killers, God gave him peace so he was able to lie down and sleep. And when he woke, he thanked God for sustaining him. He was energized.

If you're worrying about something, give that concern to God. Tell Him you're leaving that situation in His big and capable hands. Then take your hands off. Quit trying to fix the situation yourself. God can do more in minutes than we can do in years of worrying and trying to fix it. He knows what to do. Why do we think we need to worry to help God? It's fruitless.

Lord Jesus, I put my situation in Your hands now.
I choose to completely trust You to work in this and
bring about Your plan and purpose. Thank You! Amen.

# He Hears and Answers You

*I cried aloud to the Lord, and he answered me from his holy hill.*

PSALM 3:4 ESV

David cried aloud to the Lord. God knows our thoughts, so we don't have to necessarily pray aloud. But in his desperation, David did.

Sometimes we feel like crying aloud to God too. And He's all right with that. There is something therapeutic about it too.

It doesn't really matter *how* we pray to Him, but it is important to talk to God in the way you are most comfortable. He's waiting, and He loves to hear your voice. Don't hesitate to speak to Him.

You may think, *I don't want to say that. What will God think about me if I tell Him that?* Friend, He already knows. And it doesn't matter. He loves you anyway. He wants to help you through this thing you're going through.

Father, thank You that when I call on You, You answer. Help me to never hesitate to do that. In the name of Jesus, amen.

# We Are Set Free

*There is therefore now no condemnation for those who are in Christ Jesus. For the law of the Spirit of life has set you free in Christ Jesus from the law of sin and death.*

ROMANS 8:1–2 ESV

---

If you are filled with condemnation today, let it go. When Jesus is your Savior, there is no need for condemnation. He has set you free from the law of sin and death. You have a new heart and a renewed spirit.

Condemnation is not from God. Send it away and refuse to let it remain in your heart and mind. Perhaps you have done something that you feel some guilt over. Your heavenly Father is willing and ready to accept your apologies. Tell Him you're sorry and then move on. He always has forgiveness and grace for you.

Father, I send condemnation away in the name of Jesus. Thank You for freedom from the law of sin and death. You have made me new and given me a pure heart. I praise You! Amen.

# *You Have His Strength*

*I have the strength to face all conditions*
*by the power that Christ gives me.*
PHILIPPIANS 4:13 GNT

---

God did not create us and then sit up there in heaven just watching to see if we're going to mess up. No. He is with us at all times, giving us the strength to face everything that comes our way. We have the power of the Holy Spirit abiding in us, giving us courage and strength.

We don't have to face these things alone. Over and over again His Word says this. So why do we fear? We need to lean on Him and let Him make us strong and courageous. We have everything we need to succeed. We can do this!

Father, thank You for giving me the power of the Holy Spirit that dwells in me at all times, giving me the strength to face everything in life. I worship You and magnify You today. You are a good Father. Amen.

# *He Keeps Every Promise*

*"Now my time has come to die. Every one of you knows in his heart and soul that the LORD your God has given you all the good things that He promised. Every promise He made has been kept; not one has failed."*

---

It was Joshua's time to die. He was giving his farewell address to the people. He reminded them that God had given them all the good things He had promised. Every promise He had made had been fulfilled. Not one thing had He missed.

He is the same God today. His promises are still good. His heart is full of love toward you. He can be trusted. What He did for Joshua and his people, He will do for you today. Put your hope and trust in Him.

Heavenly Father, thank You for being the same God today as You were with Joshua. I put my hope and trust in You today. In Jesus' name, amen.

# See How Good He Is

*Find out for yourself how good the LORD is. Happy are those who find safety with him. Honor the LORD, all His people; those who obey him have all they need.*

PSALM 34:8–9 GNT

Sometimes we doubt His goodness. How that must make Him grieve. Over and over again in His Word, it says how good He is. This verse says to find out for yourself how good He is. How do we do that? By putting our hope and trust in Him. We will find safety in Him and be happy.

If we honor and obey Him, His Word says we will have everything we need. He provides. Always. So find out for yourself how good God is today. Put your hope and trust in Him. He's ready to show you His love.

Father, thank You for always being with me, giving me provision and protection as well as everything else that I need. I trust You today. Amen.

# Even in Old Age

*I have been young, and now am old, yet I have not seen the righteous forsaken or his children begging for bread.*

PSALM 37:25 ESV

---

No matter how old you are, God's provisions and promises don't change. The psalmist David said he had been young and now was old, yet he had never seen the righteous forsaken or his children begging for food.

God is the same today as He was then. He never changes. He's the same yesterday, today, and forever (Hebrews 13:8). His children are important to Him. Your needs will be met. You can trust Him with that. So when you're tempted to worry about the future, just change your thoughts of worry to praises to God for His faithfulness. That truly is walking by faith, not by sight.

Heavenly Father, I choose to walk by faith and not by sight today. I praise and thank You that all my needs are met according to Your riches in glory through Christ Jesus. I will not worry because I trust You. I believe You are always faithful. Amen.

# He Is Your Helper

*Commit everything you do to the LORD.*
*Trust him, and he will help you.*
PSALM 37:5 NLT

---

If you're alone today and feel overwhelmed with your situation, here's some encouragement for you: You are never alone. He is always with you. Commit everything to Him, and He will help you. He promised. What do you need help with today? Nothing is too hard for Him. He created the whole universe. He made you. He knows you inside and out. He loves you so much. Pour your heart out to Him and put your hope and trust in Him. Release those thoughts of worry and despair. Feel His peace cover you. Feel His arms surround you. He's here. He's with you right now.

Father, I choose to pour my heart out to You. I give You all my needs and concerns. I leave them in Your hands today. I trust You are working in these situations. You don't want me to worry, so I am not going to. Amen.

# He Is Our Rescuer

*The LORD rescues the godly; he is their fortress in times of trouble. The LORD helps them, rescuing them from the wicked. He saves them, and they find shelter in him.*

PSALM 37:39–40 NLT

---

If anyone knew about being rescued by the Lord, it was the psalmist David. Many times he found himself in dire need of protection. But he always found the Lord to be faithful.

So take comfort in this scripture today. Most of us aren't in quite the desperate situation David was in. But if he could trust God, certainly we can too. Stay at peace today. Give your worries to God. Give your hopeless feelings to Him. He will fill you with hope and give you the certainty that He has you in His hands. He loves you. You can find shelter and help through Him today.

Father God, thank You for being my protector and my rescuer. Thank You for bringing me out of my hopelessness into feelings of hope and peace. I trust You today. Amen.

# He's Your Supplier

*The LORD is my shepherd; I have all that I need.*
PSALM 23:1 NLT

---

A shepherd will watch over his sheep at all times. He watches for enemies who might attack the sheep. And if needed, he will defend them. He takes care of the sick and wounded ones, and he searches for the ones that are lost. He leads them by waters and places for nourishment.

The Lord is our Shepherd. We have everything that we need. He looks out for us and provides protection as well. If we learn to listen to His still, small voice, we will find that He is always there to give us direction. And if we don't listen, we may find ourselves in some trouble. Even then, He loves us and will come rescue us. He's the Good Shepherd.

Father, thank You for being my Good Shepherd
and for providing all that I need. You're a protective
and compassionate heavenly Father. Amen.

# He Gives Rest to the Weary

*He lets me rest in green meadows;*
*he leads me beside peaceful streams.*
PSALM 23:2 NLT

---

Imagine a beautiful meadow with a peaceful stream running through it. Doesn't it sound heavenly? That's what your heavenly Father wants to provide for you. A life of rest in Him, with daily peace, fully trusting Him to provide everything you need.

Maybe you're not there yet. You're not quite able to get into that rest and peace. Be encouraged by this: the Bible speaks of "laboring" into rest (Hebrews 4:9–11 KJV). You just may need to try harder to get into that place of rest—not with more work but with renewing your mind. Take control of your thoughts. Don't entertain worry and anxiety. Know who your shepherd is and relax in His presence and provision.

> Lord, I enter into rest today. I choose to entertain
> thoughts of peace and contentment, knowing
> that You are my shepherd and You are leading and
> guiding me where I need to be. I trust You. Amen.

# He Is My Strength

*He renews my strength. He guides me along*
*right paths, bringing honor to his name.*
PSALM 23:3 NLT

---

Are you tired? Weary of the battle? God is your strength giver. Go to Him for rest, renewal, and power. Then when you're refreshed and ready, He will continue to guide you in the direction you should go, bringing honor to Him.

Doing this daily develops a personal relationship with the Lord. And in doing so, we bring honor to His name. We show those around us how awesome God is by letting them witness the goodness of God in our lives. He deserves all the honor and praise.

Lord, thank You for giving me strength today.
I bring You honor and glory for everything that You
do in my life. Thank You for loving me in spite of
my weaknesses. I totally trust You today to provide
everything that I need. Help me to be a witness to those
around me of Your goodness. I worship You. Amen.

# He Is Close to Me

*Even when I walk through the darkest valley,*
*I will not be afraid, for you are close beside me.*
*Your rod and your staff protect and comfort me.*

PSALM 23:4 NLT

None of us like the thought of going through a dark valley. But inevitably we will experience some of these things during life. Even so, we can rest assured that even in the darkest valley, we do not need to be afraid. For God is close to us at those times. He will always be there to protect and comfort us.

Don't worry about it now. You don't need the grace for it now. When you need the grace, He will give it to you. Don't borrow trouble from tomorrow.

Father, thank You that You are always close beside me. Even though I walk through dark valleys, I will not be afraid because You will be right there with me. And I won't borrow trouble from tomorrow and try to figure it out now. You know the plan, and I will trust You. In Jesus' name, amen.

# *He Honors Me*

*You prepare a feast for me in the presence of my
enemies. You honor me by anointing my head
with oil. My cup overflows with blessings.*

PSALM 23:5 NLT

---

Even with David's enemies all around him, God provided a
feast for him. Then the Lord honored him by anointing his
head with oil and causing him to overflow with blessings.

Anointing someone's head with oil signified that the
person was set apart to serve God. It was a symbol of the
holy and honored calling that God was placing on their life.
David was called a man after God's own heart (1 Samuel
13:14; Acts 13:22).

No matter what failures David had in his past, God
still adored him and provided for him. He will do the same
for you. He has set you apart to serve and honor Him. He
wants to bless you and use you for His kingdom.

David's cup overflowed with blessings. That's God
heart for you too.

**Father, thank You for honoring and blessing me.
I choose to honor You and give You my best. Amen.**

# His Unfailing Love Will Pursue You

*Surely your goodness and unfailing love will pursue me all the days of my life, and I will live in the house of the LORD forever.*

PSALM 23:6 NLT

Picture God's goodness and unfailing love running after you, pursuing you every day of your life. Why would we not want to live for someone who loves us so very much? In surrendering to Him, we are assured of living in the house of the Lord forever. Heaven is our eternal home. And the Bible says it's better than any human can even imagine.

So submit to Him today. Give Him everything. Total surrender to Him is a wonderful place to be. You'll never be sorry.

Lord, I surrender to You today. Thank You for Your goodness and unfailing love. Help me to daily live in love and admiration for You as a thankful offering for all that You have done for me. I love You, Lord! Amen.

# He Will Feed and Clothe You

*"That is why I tell you not to worry about everyday life—whether you have enough food and drink, or enough clothes to wear. Isn't life more than food, and your body more than clothing? Look at the birds. They don't plant or harvest or store food in barns, for your heavenly Father feeds them. And aren't you far more valuable to him than they are?"*

MATTHEW 6:25–26 NLT

---

Jesus told us not to worry about everyday needs—things like food and clothes. Life is more than that. There's a bigger picture here.

He told the disciples to look at the birds. They don't plant and harvest and store up food in barns. They daily find the food they need. God takes care of them. And then Jesus said, "Aren't you far more valuable to him than they are?"

Trust Him today and every day. Put your hope and faith in Him. He cares for you.

Thank You, heavenly Father, for caring for me and providing for me in every way that I need it. Amen.

# Worrying Does No Good

*"Can all your worries add a single moment to your life? And why worry about your clothing? Look at the lilies of the field and how they grow. They don't work or make their clothing, yet Solomon in all his glory was not dressed as beautifully as they are. And if God cares so wonderfully for the wildflowers that are here today and thrown into the fire tomorrow, he will certainly care for you. Why do you have so little faith?"*

MATTHEW 6:27–30 NLT

---

Jesus was telling it like it really is, wasn't He? He said to look at the flowers in the field and how they grow. They don't work or make their clothing. God does it all. And look how beautiful they are!

If God cares so much for the wildflowers that last a few days at the most, He certainly will care for you.

**Lord, increase my faith. Help me to stop worrying and put my hope in You. Amen.**

# Your Father
# Already Knows

> *"So don't worry about these things, saying, 'What will we eat? What will we drink? What will we wear?' These things dominate the thoughts of unbelievers, but your heavenly Father already knows all your needs."*
>
> MATTHEW 6:31–32 NLT

---

Your Father already knows what you need. He knows every single thing about it. Unbelievers worry and fret, but we as believers should not. If we truly know the heart of our heavenly Father and trust Him, we should not have anxiety about our daily life. He has promised that He will take care of us and supply all our needs according to His riches and glory in Christ Jesus.

So trust Him completely. Thank Him in faith. Put your hope in the Lord. He is for you, not against you.

Thank You, Father, that You already know my needs. Because You do, I completely trust You today to take care of everything in my life. I will live my life as a love offering to You in thanksgiving for everything You do and provide. Amen.

# His Glorious Riches

*And this same God who takes care of me will*
*supply all your needs from his glorious riches,*
*which have been given to us in Christ Jesus.*

PHILIPPIANS 4:19 NLT

Paul was saying here to the Philippians that the same God who took care of him and supplied all of his needs would take care of them as well. And this truth is for us today. He will supply all your needs from his glorious riches. He owns the cattle on a thousand hills (Psalm 50:10).

He is our heavenly Father. We have been given His glorious riches through Christ Jesus. God, our Father, took care of everything we would ever need through the death, burial, and resurrection of His Son, Jesus Christ. The work is finished. We can rest in His love and provision. Choose to do that today.

Father, I choose to rest in Your love and provision today. Thank You for meeting all my needs according to Your glorious riches. In Jesus' name, amen.

# He Gives Plenty

*And God will generously provide all you need.*
*Then you will always have everything you need*
*and plenty left over to share with others.*

2 CORINTHIANS 9:8 NLT

---

You don't have to just *hope* God will take care of you. He promised to do so. His Word even says that He will *generously* provide all you need. You'll have everything you need plus plenty left over to share with others. This is beautiful.

Because we as believers should have everything we need plus some left over, we should be generous with everything we have. Practicing generosity is as important as it is wonderful. Even if you start out just giving something small, you will feel gratified and happy about it. Then you'll find increasing joy as you give more and more. In addition, caring for others takes our minds off ourselves and our own problems. It reminds us that life is not just about us.

Heavenly Father, I thank You for giving to me
in abundance so that I can be generous and
give to others. In Jesus' name, amen.

# When I'm Overwhelmed

*From the ends of the earth, I cry to you for help
when my heart is overwhelmed. Lead me to the
towering rock of safety, for you are my safe refuge,
a fortress where my enemies cannot reach me.*

PSALM 61:2–3 NLT

---

The psalmist David felt overwhelmed, and sometimes we do too. David cried out to the Lord for help, and we can learn from his example. He knew God was his hope. And God is our only hope too. Friends and family can't always be there for us. In fact, they will fail us sometimes, even if they have the best intentions. But God will always be with us and will never fail us. He will comfort and protect us and be a fortress when others may be mistreating us.

Let God comfort you today. Take refuge in Him.

Father, thank You for being there for me when I feel
overwhelmed and hopeless. I will run to You when
I have these feelings and let You be my comfort.
You are my everything. In Jesus' name, amen.

# He's Always Faithful

*Trust in the LORD and do good. Then you will live safely in the land and prosper. Take delight in the LORD, and he will give you your heart's desires. Commit everything you do to the LORD. Trust him, and he will help you.*

PSALM 37:3–5 NLT

These verses tell us how to live. If we trust God and do good for others, He says we will live safely and be prosperous. And if we delight in Him, He will give us our heart's desires. Then He says to commit everything we do to Him, and He'll help us.

Do we really believe this? Or do we explain it away by saying that's not what we've experienced? Wouldn't it be better to believe the Word of God than to look at our life and explain away His promises?

Let's take God at His word. What He says is true. He means it. What a wonderful God!

> Father, help me to not explain away Your
> Word. Help me to take it at face value and
> believe it. In Jesus' name, amen.

# His Unfailing Love and Faithfulness

*Your unfailing love, O LORD, is as vast as the heavens;*
*your faithfulness reaches beyond the clouds.*

PSALM 36:5 NLT

---

We cannot even grasp the vastness of God's unfailing love and faithfulness. This verse says His love and faithfulness are bigger than the heavens and go beyond the clouds. And His love is unfailing. It never runs out.

Why do we ever doubt Him? Maybe because things don't happen in our timing or just the way we had everything planned. But God knows everything. He knows what's best. And since His heart is full of love for us, why don't we just trust His timing? We are human and imperfect. But He knows all of that too. And He loves us still.

Heavenly Father, I'm so grateful that You love me in spite of my failings and human frailties. Help me to always remember and come back to the truth that Your love is unfailing and Your faithfulness reaches beyond the clouds. You are worthy of my hope and trust. Amen.

# *He Will Sustain You*

*Give your burdens to the LORD, and he will take care of you. He will not permit the godly to slip and fall.*

PSALM 55:22 NLT

---

Do your burdens feel heavy today? Do you feel in need of hope? Give your burdens to the Lord, and He will take care of you. If you belong to the Father, He will sustain you and never let you slip and fall.

He promises to take care of you. Remind yourself that He is in love with you and cares for you deeply. He will give you hope when you feel hopeless. He will give you strength when you feel weak. He will give you direction when you are confused about what to do next. He is your constant guide.

Father God, thank You for always sustaining me and taking care of every situation in my life. Thank You that You never let me fall. I'm leaning on You today and trusting You with everything. Thank You, Father!

# His Goodness and Loving-Kindness

*But when the goodness and loving kindness of God our Savior appeared, he saved us, not because of works done by us in righteousness, but according to his own mercy, by the washing of regeneration and renewal of the Holy Spirit, whom He poured out on us richly through Jesus Christ our Savior, so that being justified by his grace we might become heirs according to the hope of eternal life.*

TITUS 3:4–7 ESV

---

Our heavenly Father, because of His great love and mercy toward us, sent His only Son to die so that we might be saved from sin. Jesus died a sinner's death in our place, even though He lived a perfect life and had no sin. Oh, what love! How can we not offer Him our total surrender?

**Jesus, I thank You for Your great love and mercy to me. Because of Your death on the cross so that I might have forgiveness of sins, I have great hope and assurance of eternity in heaven with You. Thank You, Lord! Amen.**

# *Stay Steady*

*Put your hope in the LORD. Travel steadily along
his path. He will honor you by giving you the
land. You will see the wicked destroyed.*

PSALM 37:34 NLT

---

When you feel despair and hopelessness, stop and put
your focus on the Lord. Stay steady in your walk with
Him. He is always working for the good of those who love
Him, and He will honor you.

The wicked may seem to be prospering while we believers are not. But the wicked will be destroyed in the end.
And we as His children will receive our reward eventually
and eternally. So stay hopeful. Trust Him and have faith.
It pays to keep your hope and trust in the Lord. He is the
only one who never fails.

Lord, thank You for helping me to keep my hope in
You. I will not be discouraged by what I see going on
in the world. I will trust You and know that Your plans
are being fulfilled. Your will is being accomplished.
I completely trust in You. In Jesus' name, amen.

# Fear Not

*"For I hold you by your right hand—I, the LORD your God.*
*And I say to you, 'Don't be afraid. I'm here to help you.'"*

ISAIAH 41:13 NLT

---

No more comforting words can be found than these. When afraid or when you feel alone, there are no better words you could hear than your heavenly Father saying to you, "I hold you by your right hand, so don't be afraid. I'm here to help you."

But how often do we argue with God as if He doesn't understand or know what we're going through? It's a good thing He doesn't give up on us in despair. Through it all, He is ever so patient and kind, continually drawing us to Him.

Heavenly Father, thank You for being patient with me. I'm sorry when I don't take You at Your word. Help me to grow in my faith and confidence in You. I choose to put all my hope and trust in You. In Jesus' name, amen.

# He Forgives and Heals

*Let all that I am praise the LORD; with my whole heart,
I will praise his holy name. Let all that I am praise the
LORD; may I never forget the good things he does for
me. He forgives all my sins and heals all my diseases.*

PSALM 103:1–3 NLT

---

Too often, we forget all the good things God has already done for us. And we begin to grumble and complain. But when the Holy Spirit draws us back and we remember the promises of God, we lift our voices up in praise for all of His goodness.

So with our whole hearts we should praise the Lord and regularly remember all the good things He has done for us. He has forgiven all our sins, and He heals all our diseases. This is the heart of our Father. Believe Him. Trust Him. He is good.

**Father God, thank You for forgiving all my sins
and healing all my diseases. I stand in faith today
and believe Your Word for what it says. Amen.**

# He Fills My Life with Good Things

*He redeems me from death and crowns me with*
*love and tender mercies. He fills my life with good*
*things. My youth is renewed like the eagle's!*

PSALM 103:4–5 NLT

---

Many of us try very hard to stay looking young. That's why
these verses should be great news. God promises to renew
our youth like the eagle's. Godly living has its benefits.

He redeems us from death. He crowns us with love
and tender mercies. He fills our life with good things. Who
wouldn't want to put their hope and trust in a heavenly
Father with such a loving heart toward mankind?

Living for God has benefits. He isn't in heaven thinking
up things to make our life hard. He's wanting good things
for us. He loves us so much. The least we can do is to live
our lives wholeheartedly for Him in total surrender.

**Father, I totally surrender to You. I trust You and know**
**that Your desires for me are good. Thank You. Amen.**

# God Is Our Refuge and Strength

*God is our refuge and strength, always ready to help in times of trouble. So we will not fear when earthquakes come and the mountains crumble into the sea. Let the oceans roar and foam. Let the mountains tremble as the waters surge!*
PSALM 46:1–3 NLT

It's pretty scary to go through a hurricane, tornado, or earthquake. None of us would choose to do it, but it's just a matter of fact that sometimes weather conditions bring these storms. God doesn't want us to fear, though, no matter how bad storms might be. He has promised to be our refuge and strength, always helping us in times of trouble.

So next time you find yourself in one of these situations, speak to that storm and rebuke it in Jesus' name. Trust Him that no harm will come near you or your family. Stand strong in faith. He is your protection.

Thank You, Lord Jesus, that You are my protector in the midst of any kind of storm I face. I trust You. In Jesus' name, amen.

# Job Believed in God

*"But as for me, I know that my Redeemer lives, and he will stand upon the earth at last. And after my body has decayed, yet in my body I will see God! I will see him for myself. Yes, I will see him with my own eyes. I am overwhelmed at the thought!"*

JOB 19:25–27 NLT

---

We've all heard of the patience of Job. While he was in the midst of his trials, he had to be hoping God would stop all the persecution. And even though his suffering didn't stop when he may have wished, he remained faithful to God.

At the end, he stood strong and said, "I know that my Redeemer lives, and. . .I will see Him with my own eyes." He was even overwhelmed, and he rejoiced when he thought of seeing the Lord.

**Father, in the midst of all my trials and tribulations, help me to remain firm and strong in my faith, knowing that in the end I will see You. And it will be worth it all. Amen.**

# The Great Hope of the Believer

*Even though I walk through the valley of the shadow of death, I will fear no evil, for you are with me; your rod and your staff, they comfort me.*

PSALM 23:4 ESV

---

Even when David faced death, he said he would not be afraid, because he knew God was close to him. And so it is with us. When we face death, we will not be alone. God is with us now, and He will be with us then.

If we are believers in Jesus Christ, we do not need to fear. Death is not a destination but a journey. We go from this life to the next one. And we are never alone in this journey.

Heaven is a beautiful place. So do not fear death. We have great things in store for us. Our hope is in the resurrection. Praise God!

**Heavenly Father, I'm grateful that even though I go through the valley of the shadow of death, I need not fear any evil, because You are with me. Amen.**

# *His Provision*

*Fear the LORD, you his godly people, for those
who fear him will have all they need. Even strong
young lions sometimes go hungry, but those who
trust in the LORD will lack no good thing.*

PSALM 34:9–10 NLT

---

Are you in a desperate place today, hoping for your needs
to be supplied? Fear not. The Lord has promised to provide for you. He says those who love and respect Him
will have everything that they need. And they will lack
no good thing.

So tell Him exactly what you need. He already knows,
but it's good to pour your heart out to God. In that way,
you surrender to Him and put your faith in Him.

Then remember that you left that burden in His hands,
and trust that He will take care of it. He is good, and He
always keeps His word.

Father, thank You that I don't have to worry.
I put my trust and hope in You knowing that
You keep Your promises. You know what I
need, and I trust You to provide. Amen.

# All Will Be Well with You

*Blessed is everyone who fears the LORD, who walks in his ways! You shall eat the fruit of the labor of your hands; you shall be blessed, and it shall be well with you.*

PSALM 128:1–2 ESV

---

We are promised to be blessed if we love and respect the Lord. If we walk in His ways, He said that all will be well.

God wants good things for us. He is loving and generous, and we can put our hope and trust fully in Him.

The more we get this truth ingrained in our hearts and minds, the more we will be able to trust Him completely. Meditate on this scripture. Become totally convinced of the goodness of your heavenly Father.

> Lord, I'm grateful for Your goodness and for Your promises to bless me. I choose to walk in Your ways. Please guide me in them. I praise You and offer You my life in exchange for everything You have done for me. Amen.

# He Watches Over You

*Behold, the eye of the LORD is on those who fear him,*
*on those who hope in his steadfast love, that he may deliver*
*their soul from death and keep them alive in famine.*

PSALM 33:18–19 ESV

Our God is always watching over us. If you have hope in His steadfast love, He will protect you and deliver you from death and keep you alive in famine. In other words, He has provision for you regardless of your circumstances. It doesn't matter how desperate things get in your life, He will be there for you and take care of you. His grace will be sufficient.

Don't even entertain thoughts of "what if?" You don't need to go there. He promised. He provides. He's faithful. You can depend on Him. Put your hope and trust in Him today.

Father, I thank You that I can trust You no matter what my situation is. You promised to take care of me every step of the way. I put my trust in You today. Amen.

# Long Life Is Promised

*The fear of the LORD prolongs life,*
*but the years of the wicked will be short.*

PROVERBS 10:27 ESV

---

To fear the Lord does not mean to be afraid of Him but to have awe and respect for Him. When we live with awe and respect for the Lord, it will add years to our lives. Good living pays. There are benefits.

Living according to God's will is the right way to live. He created us and knows what is best for us. And if we follow His principles, we will find peace and good health. There are reasons for following God's Word, so get into it regularly and find out what His plans are for daily life.

Father, I choose to be in Your Word, and I want to learn more about Your plans for daily living. I will follow Your ways and live according to Your will and purpose for me. Thank You for revealing them to me as I spend time in Your Word. Increase my understanding of Your will. In Jesus' name, amen.

# His Love and Salvation Extend Down Through Generations

*But the love of the LORD remains forever with those who fear him. His salvation extends to the children's children of those who are faithful to his covenant, of those who obey his commandments!*

PSALM 103:17–18 NLT

---

God honors your holy life even down to the generations who follow you. His salvation extends to your children's children to those who are faithful to obey Him.

If you're concerned about your children or grandchildren, continue to honor God with your own life. Be a good example to your family. Surrender your family members to the Lord, and trust Him to reach them. God will honor your faith. And until you see those promises fulfilled, thank God daily in faith for what He has promised. Trust Him. Put your hope in Him for your family. He is faithful.

Father, I'm so grateful that You are working in my family. I trust You to work in all the children important in my life, and may they all honor You wholeheartedly. In Jesus' name, amen.

# Hope of Forgiveness of Sin

*But people are counted as righteous, not because of their work, but because of their faith in God who forgives sinners.*

ROMANS 4:5 NLT

---

We have this blessed hope of forgiveness for our sins. And we are forgiven, not because of our works or anything that we have done but because of our faith in the Lord Jesus who died for us. He did the work for us because we could never be good enough. He was the perfect sacrifice.

So all we have to do is believe in Him, and He cleanses us from all unrighteousness. Then we become the righteousness of God. This is a wonderful hope. A wonderful truth. We can never be perfect. And God knows that. So thank God today that you are counted as righteous if you have believed in Him.

Father, thank You for counting me as righteous because of my faith in Jesus and His work on the cross. Thank You for that wonderful gift. Amen.

# He Gives Rest to the Weary

*Then Jesus said, "Come to me, all of you who are weary and carry heavy burdens, and I will give you rest. Take my yoke upon you. Let me teach you, because I am humble and gentle at heart, and you will find rest for your souls. For my yoke is easy to bear, and the burden I give you is light."*

MATTHEW 11:28–30 NLT

---

Jesus is gentle and humble at heart. If we come to Him with our heavy burdens and our weariness, He will give us rest. He said He would teach us. His yoke is easy and the burden is light. It's not hard to serve Jesus. It is the best and most peaceful way to live.

**In Your name, Jesus, I come to You with all my weariness and heavy burdens. And I take Your yoke and ask You to teach me Your ways. Thank You, Lord. Amen.**

# Hope of Our Inheritance

*Furthermore, because we are united with Christ, we have received an inheritance from God, for he chose us in advance, and he makes everything work out according to his plan.*

EPHESIANS 1:11 NLT

---

Because we have been born of His Spirit, we receive an inheritance from God. We have hope of life everlasting and a home in heaven. And until that comes to pass, we can trust that He will work everything out according to His plan and for our good if we follow Him.

Trust Him with your life—every detail. He knows best and will guide you every step of the way. Every morning turn to Him and give Him your day. Ask for His direction. Then listen for His voice. He will speak to you.

Heavenly Father, I choose to ask for Your direction, and I listen for Your voice so that I can get instruction from You for my daily life. I want to follow Your plan. In Jesus' name, amen.

# Hope for His Direction

*The LORD says, "I will guide you along the best pathway for your life. I will advise you and watch over you."*

PSALM 32:8 NLT

---

It's not hard to find God's plan. He plainly says He will guide us along the best pathway for our life. And it is not His intention to make it hard to figure out. We sometimes make it so difficult, but He clearly says He will advise us and watch over us.

We can have hope for God's direction for our future. And we can trust that He will equip us for whatever He calls us to do. It will be a joyous journey! He does not want us to be miserable.

> Father, I thank You that I can trust You to show me Your perfect plan for my life. I believe You will give me direction and lead me on a path that will be the best thing for me. Amen.

# The Hope of Freedom

*Jesus said to the people who believed in him,
"You are truly my disciples if you remain
faithful to my teachings. And you will know
the truth, and the truth will set you free."*

JOHN 8:31–32 NLT

---

Knowing the truth will set us free. *Knowing* is a key word there.

In order to know the truth, we have to be following the Lord and reading His Word. We must remain faithful to God and follow His teachings.

The way we know the truth is by being in His Word. This takes discipline. So set some time aside every day to read the Word of God and talk to Him. And don't just talk to Him; stop and listen for Him to speak to you as well. Conversation goes both ways.

**Thank You, Lord, that I can have the hope
of true freedom in Christ. Amen.**

# The Hope of Our Inheritance

*In him you also, when you heard the word of truth, the gospel of your salvation, and believed in him, were sealed with the promised Holy Spirit, who is the guarantee of our inheritance until we acquire possession of it, to the praise of his glory.*
EPHESIANS 1:13–14 ESV

---

We have this great hope of our inheritance through Jesus Christ, our Savior. When we heard the truth and believed in Him, we received the Holy Spirit, who gives us assurance of our inheritance. So we look forward with great hope to our eternal home in heaven, where we will be forever with Jesus.

Following the Lord here on this earth has great benefits. But we also have an eternal home waiting for us. And God's Word says that no man can even imagine its beauty (1 Corinthians 2:9). We can't even fathom what it will be like. We wait in anticipation for that day.

**Lord Jesus, thank You for the eternal hope of my inheritance in heaven. Amen.**

# The Promises of Abraham Belong to Us

*And now that you belong to Christ, you are the*
*true children of Abraham. You are his heirs,*
*and God's promise to Abraham belongs to you.*

When we became believers in Jesus Christ, God made us heirs of Abraham. And because we are Abraham's offspring, we are heirs to all the promises God gave to Abraham. Anything and everything that we need has been provided for. This gives us great hope.

God blessed Abraham immensely, and He will do the same for you. Go back to Genesis and read about Abraham. Find out how God blessed him. Then thank Him in faith for blessing you as well. In return, be determined to bless others through your blessings. God desires for us to be generous givers.

Lord, thank You that I am the seed of Abraham,
and all Your promises to Abraham apply to
me as well. Help me to be a good steward of
every blessing that You give to me. Amen.

# You Are God's Own Child

*Now you are no longer a slave but God's own child.*
*And since you are his child, God has made you his heir.*

GALATIANS 4:7 NLT

---

If we really know that we are God's children, there is no reason to feel hopeless and in despair. He has promised so much for us. We are no longer slaves but His very own children! And because we are His children, we are heirs to His kingdom. We have a great inheritance to look forward to.

While life may bring its trials, He has promised to get us through every one of them. And eternity is going to be glorious. Can you imagine walking on streets of gold? Can you imagine singing in the heavenly choir? Can you imagine living in a mansion? Can you imagine being with your loved ones who have gone on before you? These are just a few of the things that we have to look forward to.

**Father, I praise You for the hope of my future. Amen.**

# He's Always with You

*"What's more, I am with you, and I will protect you wherever you go. One day I will bring you back to this land. I will not leave you until I have finished giving you everything I have promised you."*

GENESIS 28:15 NLT

---

Jacob was having a dream, and the Lord spoke these words to him. When he awoke, he realized that he had been in the presence of God.

Even though this was spoken to Jacob, this shows the heart of our Father. He will do the same for us. He will never leave us and will protect us wherever we go.

Spend some time with Him today and let Him assure you that He will do the same for you. We can put our hope and trust in God because He will never fail.

Father, thank You for giving me so many examples in the scriptures to see Your heart. You don't play favorites. You will provide for and protect me today, just as You have always done for Your people in the past. I'm so grateful! Amen.

# *No One Can Stand Against You*

*"No one will be able to stand against you as long as you live. For I will be with you as I was with Moses. I will not fail you or abandon you."*

JOSHUA 1:5 NLT

---

You may feel alone today, but you are never alone. God promised to always be with you and never fail or abandon you. And no one will be able to stand against you, because He is there to defend you. Can you picture Him standing with you, ready to fight for you, right now? The almighty God of the universe! What a beautiful thought.

So never fear. When those thoughts of fear come into your mind, send them away. Speak the name of Jesus, and remember He is with you every moment of every day.

Father God, thank You for always being with me and promising to never fail or abandon me. You are standing with me, and no one can come against me. You are here to defend me. Thank You, Lord. Amen.

# Hope for Difficult Times

*"When you go through deep waters, I will be with you. When you go through rivers of difficulty, you will not drown. When you walk through the fire of oppression, you will not be burned up; the flames will not consume you."*

ISAIAH 43:2 NLT

---

No one said life would be a bed of roses. We live in a fallen world filled with sin. Things will happen to us that are not pleasant. They might even be awful. But we can count on the fact that God will be with us no matter what we have to endure in this life. And none of these situations will defeat us.

Because we have the Holy Spirit with us, we are more than conquerors through Him who gave His life for us. We are overcomers. And we need not fear. He is with us.

Father, I'm so grateful that no matter what I go through, You will be there to lift me up and carry me through it. No situation can defeat me. I am an overcomer through Christ who strengthens me. Amen.

# Who We Are in Christ

*But you are not like that, for you are a chosen
people. You are royal priests, a holy nation,
God's very own possession. As a result, you can
show others the goodness of God, for he called you
out of the darkness into his wonderful light.*

1 PETER 2:9 NLT

---

We have been redeemed. We are God's chosen people.
And because of this, we can show the world the goodness of God. He has brought us out of darkness into His
wonderful light. The world is looking for answers to their
problems. And we have the answer.

We can hold our heads up high and know that we are
the redeemed of the Lord. And because of that, we can
overcome any situation that comes our way. He has made
us to be victorious in Christ.

Father, I thank You that I have been redeemed. Help me
to show others Your goodness and bring them into Your
wonderful light. In the name of Jesus I pray, amen.

# His Grace Is All I Need

*Each time he said, "My grace is all you need. My power works best in weakness." So now I am glad to boast about my weaknesses, so that the power of Christ can work through me.*

2 CORINTHIANS 12:9 NLT

---

If you're feeling weak today and troubled in your spirit, know that Jesus said His grace is all you need. His power works best in your weakness. Turn it all over to God and trust Him. He will come through for you. When you are weak, He is strong. The power of Christ will work through you, and you will overcome.

His grace is enough. He is all you need. He will take care of you and supply all your needs. Don't ever forget it!

Jesus, I believe that I can trust You when I am weak.
Your grace is sufficient. I will lean heavily against
You and trust You to come through for me with
all the power that I need. In Your name, amen.

# *Don't Be Afraid*

*But now thus says the LORD, he who created you,*
*O Jacob, he who formed you, O Israel: "Fear not, for I have*
*redeemed you; I have called you by name, you are mine."*

ISAIAH 43:1 ESV

---

They say that everyone likes to be called by their name. It's just more personable and feels more caring. If someone takes the time to actually remember your name and calls you by it, that feels good.

Isn't it wonderful that God created and formed us? And He's telling us not to fear, because He has redeemed us. What good news! But not only that. He has called us by our name and says we are His. This is beautiful.

Think on that for a moment. God, the only true God, the God of the universe, made you, redeemed you, called you by name, and says, "You are Mine!"

So don't be afraid. He's got you!

Father, thank You for creating me,
redeeming me, calling me by my name,
and telling me I'm Yours. I love You, Lord!

# We Became the Righteousness of God

*God made him who had no sin to be sin for us, so that in him we might become the righteousness of God.*

2 CORINTHIANS 5:21 NIV

---

To those of us who are in Christ Jesus, we have become the righteousness of God. He sent Jesus, His Son, who had no sin, to be sin for us. Jesus took our sin to the cross. He took the punishment that we deserved. All we have to do is believe in Him, and He will save us and deliver us from our sin.

This is the good news of the gospel! This enables us to have great hope for our future. We can live free from sin and condemnation. We can have a life of victory and joy in Jesus. There is no better news than that.

Jesus, Your death, burial, and resurrection
enable me to become the righteousness of God.
Wow! I worship You, and I put all my hope and
trust in You today. In Your name, amen.

# You Can Ask Your Father Anything

*"In that day you will no longer ask me anything.
Very truly I tell you, my Father will give you
whatever you ask in my name. Until now you have
not asked for anything in my name. Ask and you
will receive, and your joy will be complete."*

JOHN 16:23–24 NIV

---

God is generous and loving, wanting to give you good gifts.
You can put your hope in Him, knowing that He will hear
and answer your prayers. He truly desires to show love to
you. He wants to meet all your needs.

Don't ever think that you have to be perfect for God to
bless you and answer your prayers. He understands that
you are human and imperfect. We all are. He sees your
heart. And He loves you so much.

Father, thank You that I can ask You anything, and
You hear and answer my prayers. I trust You to
do what is best for me. In Jesus' name, amen.

# You Can Have Peace

*"I have told you these things, so that in me you may
have peace. In this world you will have trouble.
But take heart! I have overcome the world."*

JOHN 16:33 NIV

---

Jesus told His disciples these things so that they would
know they could have peace. He also said that in this world
they would have many troubles but to take heart. Why?
Because He had already overcome the world.

The same is true for us today. Jesus has already overcome any trouble that we could possibly face. We can
live in total peace and victory because of this. We have so
much more power available to us if we just take advantage
of it. Let's be determined to be overcomers through the
power of the Holy Spirit.

Father, I choose to be an overcomer through
the power of the Holy Spirit. I choose to live in
peace, trusting You and putting my hope and
faith in You. In the name of Jesus, amen.

# *Everything Will Work Out*

*And we know that for those who love God all things work together for good, for those who are called according to his purpose.*

ROMANS 8:28 ESV

---

As a believer, let this scripture fill you with great hope and comfort. Not everything that happens to us in life feels good. Some things are hard. Some things are hurtful. Yet we can rest in the fact that God will work all things together for our good. He will make sure that we benefit in some way from the hard and hurtful times. Perhaps it may be a lesson learned, or He may change the situation around to bless us. But whatever comes our way, we can know that our heavenly Father is aware and will use the situation for our good. This shows the loving heart of our heavenly Father.

Dear Lord, thank You that You work everything together for my good. I trust You and keep my hope and faith in You. In the name of Jesus, amen.

# Be the New You

*Since you have heard about Jesus and have learned the*
*truth that comes from him, throw off your old sinful*
*nature and your former way of life, which is corrupted*
*by lust and deception. Instead, let the Spirit renew*
*your thoughts and attitudes. Put on your new nature,*
*created to be like God—truly righteous and holy.*

EPHESIANS 4:21–24 NLT

---

When you're tempted to feel down about yourself, remember that you have thrown off your old sinful nature and your former way of life. You are not that same person anymore. You have the Holy Spirit within you. He will help you renew your thoughts and attitudes.

So be the new you who has been created in God's likeness—righteous and holy. Let the Holy Spirit change your thinking. The old person is gone. You have been made new. Hold on to this hope. Believe it.

> **Thank You, heavenly Father, that I am a new person, redeemed by the Lord. And I have the mind of Christ. In Jesus' name, amen.**

# *His Provision Is Complete*

*And my God will supply every need of yours
according to his riches in glory in Christ Jesus.*
PHILIPPIANS 4:19 ESV

No matter what your need is today, God has promised to provide for it. And He is not going to just barely take care of you. He will take care of you according to His riches in glory. And He is lacking in nothing!

So you can sit back and relax, trusting God and knowing He will provide. Worrying does no good. In fact, it is a sin. So if you find yourself worrying today, ask God to forgive you and see yourself in His big and mighty hands. He's got you!

Heavenly Father, I thank You for supplying all my needs according to Your riches in glory. Forgive me when I have doubted You and worried about my situations. I know You want me to trust You. So I totally put myself in Your care today. I believe You will provide everything I need, because You have promised, and You never fail. In Jesus' name, Amen.

# Why We Should Have Hope

*And I am sure of this, that he who began a good work in you will bring it to completion at the day of Jesus Christ.*

PHILIPPIANS 1:6 ESV

---

Sometimes we tend to think negatively about our future. We get discouraged about our maturing process. We consider the desires and goals we have and end up feeling discouraged, wondering how these things will ever happen.

But take heart, my friend. God said that what He started in you, He will finish. That's hopeful. Actually it's more than hopeful. It is God's Word, and it's certain. He never fails. We can count on Him. Do your part, and He will definitely do His.

Thank You, Lord, that I can know in the depths of my being that You will be faithful to complete in me what You started. You have a plan. I submit to You and trust You completely. Help me stand strong in my faith, do my part, and believe You always. Amen.

# God Is the Best Guide

*I will instruct you and teach you in the way you should go; I will counsel you with my eye upon you.*
PSALM 32:8 ESV

There is nothing better than having the God of the universe, who created you and knows you better than anyone, to guide you in the way you should go and give you wisdom for life. He will be your hiding place and your protection.

When life brings hard times and situations, you can go to Him for advice. He has promised to be there and watch over you. He wants you to be victorious.

And you don't have to just hope things will get better like the world hopes. You can put your hope in the one true God who is the *real source* of *all* hope. Trust Him completely, with great confidence, knowing He always keeps His word and is faithful.

Father, help me put all my hope and trust
in You completely. I lean on You for wisdom
and guidance for my life. Amen.

# He Shows Kindness and Love

*But—when God our Savior revealed his kindness and love,*
*he saved us, not because of the righteous things we had*
*done, but because of his mercy. He washed away our sins,*
*giving us a new birth and new life through the Holy Spirit.*
*He generously poured out the Spirit upon us through Jesus*
*Christ our Savior. Because of his grace he made us right in his*
*sight and gave us confidence that we will inherit eternal life.*

TITUS 3:4–7 NLT

---

The greatest kindness and love ever shown was when God sent His Son, Jesus, to die on the cross for our sins. What great mercy! We have been given a new life through the Holy Spirit. We are now the righteousness of Christ. Now we will inherit eternal life in heaven. This is the best hope!

If you don't know for certain that you have given your life to Christ, ask Him into your life right now. He will not refuse you. He loves you more than you can imagine.

**Lord Jesus, I repent of my sins and invite You to be**
**my Lord and Savior. In Your holy name, amen.**

# *About the Author*

**Sheila Thomas** lives in south Florida with her husband of more than fifty years. They have three grown children, thirteen grandchildren, and one great-grandchild. Sheila is a music teacher, pianist, vocalist, speaker, and author who uses her gifts to minister to others through social media. She has served in church in music ministry as well as women's ministry. Sheila does all this to fulfill her purpose in life, which is ministry through music, prayer, encouragement, and motivating and mentoring others.